ONE GOOD EAR

ONE GOOD EAR

Poems & Prose

M I C H A E L   F O L E Y

ISBN:978-1-7352466-0-4
Inkwells Publishing, PO Box 426, Hawi, HI 96719

For Charlotte

CONTENTS

ACKNOWLEDGMENTS

Mahalo nui loa—warm thanks—first of all to family and friends for reading many of these poems as I wrote them. I am forever grateful for your support and encouragement. Thanks to my fellow Inkwells, especially Laura Burkhart, for continuing to read and support my work. Thanks to my hula sister Lynda Wallach for requesting a poem entitled *Kupuna Hula* at the Kohala Country Fair, where I joined my fellow Inkwells writing poems on demand. Other poems, including *Think Ditch, Looking Out the Back Door, Out on the Headlands, Horses & Animals & Kohala, Double Tuberose Lei, Your Name,* and *Fishing the Hō'ea Flats* were also written in response to prompts given us by members of the public at the fair, and subsequently published in the chapbook, *Fair Requests.* Mahalo nui to my hula halau, Na Kupuna O Kohala and our beloved Kumu Kaui Nakamura and Alaka'i Michael Matsu, for coming into my life on the first evening after my wife died, bringing food, dancing hula, showing me the way forward. On the third night, by the time my family had arrived, the halau returned with their aloha, more food and more hula, and I learned what *I mua* really means. Mahalo nui loa to Kumu Keala Ching and Rolinda Bean for their guidance, inspiration, dedication and their generous invitation to all to join them in celebrating life through hula. Thanks to the Hawai'i Writers Guild for the opportunity to read several of these poems at the Kohala Public Library. I am grateful to Helena Kim and Susanna Moore for their kind words for this collection. Thanks also to Linda Petrucelli, fellow member of the Hawai'i Writers Guild and the "writing buddy" I've never met, whose email observations have given me such welcome validation.

AN ABSENCE OF GULLS

I've always lived on an island
always a sense of coastline
more water than sense more
sky than I could ever touch
before it's time to come inside
a time when minutes equal days
and cats have scales instead of fur
hold their paws to the tillers
venture out from the known
shorelines where abductions abound
in this manner sea shells become
conduits to a deeper music
the chorus serious
forming perfect hollows
the endless sound of the sea
in the mouth of a cave
flags flutter here
among candy wrappers
I never wanted
to be a day tripper
always the resident crab
scuttling in and out of the debris
believing since you're asking believing
in impermanence and no self what else
the headlines mean nothing to me now
although you might have wondered
about the lost years suffocating
in the heart of the country
out of sight of the sea

I turned my sight
to flora and fauna
muses met in the childhood garden
how the absence of gulls led me
to leaving my windows open
and shades never drawn
in hopes of hearing their cries
but not so not now I've heard
the black silence of the soaring 'iwa

A THIRD INTERPRETATION

There's a third interpretation following
the gyrations of that thief the ʻiwa
the great frigate bird who snatches
lauʻipala the yellow tang from the waves
in the waters off Maka o Hule Heiau
where navigators watch and pray

Below that hill another eye searches
for meaning an old man catches
sight of a single malolo a flying
fish leaping through flecks of white
snow the horizon broken into
a million pieces of froth or so it seems

Beneath the waning kāne moon
light softens and falls earthward
those frigid lunar mountains
crumble earthward erasing
the face or whatever our imagination
saw while the lunar arc kept lifting

Lifting I turn to a boulder smooth
enough to lay the rest of this page
my heel tangles in a spray of green
kiawe I keep asking what's this mean
I'm asking for permission for forgiveness
stopping standing writing this

My world isn't frozen anymore
words no longer links in a chain
nothing can be held down
I've made my promise to let go
stop holding the world accountable
you I say you I sing owe me

Nothing meanwhile flies buzz
merrily at my ears eyes fingers
one ant follows the broken arc
of my cuticle I will not let my
opposable thumb set me apart
this is my prayer saying let me in

To do the real work dance
with grasses wings waves
dance until secrets leap clear
of the surface as the known
line of old comes ashore
opens the eye of morning

THE KNOWN LINE OF OLD

Why do we dig so deep?
ground returns all
that was lost to the surface
every seven years or so
as with everything
this question comes up
for me if not for you

the day after Christmas
to reach Nishimura Bay
I walk through Mahukona
with its abandoned warehouses
and ruined jetties feral cats
scattering right and left
into wild brush aflame

with green blades sprung
from last week's storm
there stands Maka o Hule
the navigational heiau
whose eyes oversee
a unique threshold
the known line of old

almighty gusts of wind
leap from abrupt lava cliffs
to ride the ocean's back
and shudder north in the blizzard
of white-caps that reaches

the horizon where one 'iwa
solitary in his black cloak

scribes where calm meets tempest
gone free the rock-bound monk
whose aerial twists and turns
make a journey of wings
look so easy he reaches now
and then to nab a flash of yellow
from churning white water

standing stones high above
mark purpose and direction
although once laid aside
gun mounts instead facing
the promise of death
made by an enemy the other
side of the horizon no

miniature Stonehenge no
fence to keep picture
taking people safe from
understanding anything
Maka o Hule Heiau rides
the surface of this world
and I keep returning
asking for direction
to that other world

OLD COAST GUARD ROAD

Many's the morning I walk down
Old Coast Guard Road and today's turning
of the year makes night and day equal

the chorus of haole koa pods silent
seeds of long grasses long fallen
and at the tips of dried blades

radials and spirals of spider silk
low-slung and sequined with dewdrops
their translucent mistress still

in morning asana as my feet pass
the low velveteen spill of moss
pale green below the humming pole

where I stand still too until I
remember to look up for the return
of the northern mockingbird

SNAIL

No riddle the rocking house on the last day
of September a small thing crossed the road
winter's harbinger with her sticky iridescence
an absence of whales as yet in the distance

survived my truck wheels downhill and my
observation intent on foot the two miles
up and back but my V8 2000 rpm one gallon
of fuel spent getting home is a question

for all of us who appreciate the snail
for her contribution to the forestalling
of entropy oh life oh morning glory
just to be you—make it to the other side

THE OTHER SIDE IN THE RAIN

Thinking of the other side
in the rain I'd like to talk
with the other the one
eyed by my inner mind
the Oh! There! Sigh...or
Here? chin palm elbow
table head alea aloft
clouds soft whereabouts
suspended in mountains
nothing for the messenger
who waits but silence
all last night stillness
even the resident frog
stops his grumbling
or is he just afraid to speak
for fear the spell will break
and none of us will hear
the wind make her way
down from the precipitous
peaks over the soft shouldered
pu'us entering the house gently
through the long hair the short
the forgotten surfaces of skin
how shall I begin how can I
do I introduce myself to her?

AS IF SHE WERE

As if she were the moon he pulled gently
the stalks the stems the leaves that follow
the flowers their pistils the stamen teased
coaxed with her long ethereal fingers

day or night even when her powers waned
a slim curvature of light but she was
not the moon he realized and he
lay down with the wind in a ditch

in that thick hot summer nothing would
raise him up again it seemed all memory
of her coming were some fanciful myth
some pattern of rising and falling

following the sun she was the moon
said the wind she was not said the ditch
and he ached and he arched and sighed
and the ground cracked open looking for her

AFTER CALIBAN

After the ship broke up
and the passengers were
scattered, Shakespeare's offspring
son of a witch, Caliban said

Be not afeard: the isle is full
of noises. (But here on this
island I heard him
say "full of music")

What do you mean? Lutes? Mandolins? Modified
Spanish guitars? Their strings slackened?

No. Well, yes of course, but more
than that. I mean the sound the east wind
makes as it blows across the wires
at Puʻu Hue. I mean the cry of the unseen
goat kid lost on lava at the Great Crack
in the hour before dawn with the waves'
rush at this island's newest land. I mean
that long scratch of an owl coming
from casuarina in the dark of night.
I mean the rustling
toads in the woodpile
by the door. The clacking
of coconut palms in the slightest
breeze. The splash of one koi
in the pond. The mosquitoes'
buzz in the left ear. The murmur

of a man and a woman touching
each other for the first time
beneath the light of the moon.
The high pitch objections of the mountain
road as the boy's car takes the corners
hard and pushes through the gas pedal.

But this last (says the other),
this isn't music.

Why not? Isn't
it all a part
of the symphony?
The overture
of our days? The fall
of ice in the freezer?
The slam of the screen
door?

I'm tired of your
list.

I'm suggesting
that you just listen.

I need my own
sounds. Music
that reminds me,
cheers me up, even
music that covers
over these island
sounds you so

monotonously
drone on about.

Those sounds?
Your sounds?
These sounds, too,
are a part of it.

THE DITCH

There's something warm about surrender she heard herself say
half in water half in dream a chorus of toads one single baritone
singing his deep protest under the Muku Moon caught between

overlays of percussion rapid bamboo sections she was lost
for words and finding the right word was vital to her even
here in the direst mirest circumstances not one shadow

only ditch sounds nor even a floating lilikoi to light the way
bufo marinus she said and silence looked hard into the darkness
eyes wide open a little formal isn't it she heard a voice return

would you prefer cane toad she whispered or nameless
proliferators warts and all I beg your pardon he said
aren't you forgetting your manners no time for that she said

like the fossilized arteries of a forgotten goddess the ditch
had no beginning and no end it pulled down the stars
to dank sanctuaries crawling with dead languages

what's with overpopulation anyhow said the toad
we're all racing to the edge of the proverbial cliff
but I prefer the ditch he whispered you've got a point

she sighed perhaps I'll lie here till the smoke passes
till the haze clears till the burning fields choke
with the bitter people's ashes there's nothing subtle

there's nothing worth redeeming here be careful
said the toad I'm the victim of relocation myself
where's home my kids ask hell forget that thought

home is wherever the sky cries out and down I say
life's either a dance or a game of statues and you
take your chances out there on the tarmac

I've forgotten why she said confiding in the stranger
his implacable bodhisattva smile wide beneath
her fingertips I've lost my way I'm running

yeah dance or statues he mumbled and dropped
out of touch till dawn the world still on fire
crazy people out there with coupons and vouchers

waving flags and political placards standing
on street corners trying to make eye contact
with faceless citizens hunkered down in their bubbles

hands gripping the wheels as long as those hands
gripped the damn wheels they believed in freedom
talk about illusion she sighed and sank into a long sleep

RELOCATING TOADS

Two in the pile of cedar logs cut soon after high winds sent down
good-sized branches months ago and two more last night at dusk
singing their deep gourd fluttering song of the pond flecked green
with azolla fern and in my approach with net and light stone-still

spilled into a bucket the lid laid over till morning when in the black
truck bed they swayed and clung to the bottom circle of uncertainty
in their own piss and litter while I drove three miles to the edge
of the wet trades and no further according to conscience before

looking back once reached in four times marveling at the inscrutable
guise of their smile lines and toxic warts their lidded eyes so
unlike mine what did they see? beyond that short arc of light
as each curved away from my hand into the long grasses

mute and invisible then they waited in the margins for a sign of rain
again and again I dance this dance of moving inconveniences
to some distance remembering fairy tales and nightmares in that glance
between my place and history a repetition a tenacity of life returning

THINK DITCH

Think ditch she said
think flowing she said
think waters of life and I
thought of the trail above
White Road where the overlook
takes your breath away whether
clear day waterfalls spill
off the opposite ridge or
mist fills the known world
hides every step you have taken
to be here I remember
craning my head
into one of the tunnels up there
feeling a rush of cold air
skim past me as I called out
her name which came
back to me the following year
crazy as that sounds and every
time I crossed the ditch
in the months that followed
out in Hamakua or above Pololu
at the Five Waterfalls
even off Kahei Road
where it's not paved
by the gulch that runs
down the west side of my place
each time I listened I heard
the echo of my song

'ALALĀ RETURNS

I wake in the middle of the night squinting
as the phosphorescent hands dance ua'uhi
seems the middle of the night is moving
nobody warned me the center refuses to stay
still that I'll have to start over with my still
small voice saying *The small hand points to the hours*
until Time it seems is dancing the hula
sensuous alluring *Come on!* she beckons
swoops in front of me dressed up like
night itself celebrating the return
of 'Alalā with a flash of thigh startling me
I grab my pen for protection as panic
rains down head to toe I'm inside
the belly of an enormous sea serpent
surfacing so fast my ears are popping
She opens her mouth and I hear the ocean
breathing in great long swishing waves
This is crazy! I'm here on the island but
Time turns her back on me I look up
as Her fingers streak down the cliff face
in two streaming waterfalls I obey Her
command implicitly and swim sidestroke
as best I can across the roaring pool
the frothing chaos there's a cave if I
can reach it *No! I refuse to think like this!*
I reach it! I see the movie of my life
stretch back in animated pictures
scenes flickering with images of wild
dancing women blood pouring like thick

molasses into the sea making lots of steam
turning lots of men into helpless rocks
and at this point in the story my feet
remembering they were once capable
of gripping the edge of the world
with no uncertain degree of tenacity
begin to dance *Kaholo to the left*
welcoming air to my breast with both
hands bringing Time closer to home
just telling you this my heart beats faster
it's a dance of embrace and let go
the ultimate tease a test for the mind
you know the one who gets in the way
after all it's the middle of the night
a dance of light popping out from
inside outside trade winds make
love to the trees in figures of eight
Time's arms try keeping up She's not so
sure-footed after all it's a balancing act
an illusion She got me by the you-know-
what but by the time I get back to bed
with my clipboard and my glasses She's
disappeared so I begin again moving
the ink twisting and turning on the page
working against the clock to get born while
the image of Her terrible beauty's still fresh

WHITE OWL

—introduced to Hawaiʻi in the 1950s to control rodents, which arrived much earlier by canoe or ship

I

Rise up from your beds break your dreams
the owl paints her version as we lie sleeping
life spills open at the seams
and from her eyes night comes bleeding

dark watercolors cross the page
earth and heaven blend light erased
silent humorless she sets her stage
in one sweep of wings opened and embraced

her beak's born from the curve of ruthless intent
she's a huntress happiest with heart of prey racing
across the fields of the moon till spent
whose goddess smiles on this chasing?

dawn comes erasing this small sign
that death is nature's own design

II

Were you that white cloud
broke against a corner of my rig
traveling north of here? Night
your light hits heavy against my
no! I'm saying outloud braking and
swerving I drive on maybe a mile
lugging shuddering until I turn

find you in the high beams turn
the engine off carry you in tears
to the mown stubble in the verge
your wings fall open like God's fan
soft angelic life recent with questing
your talons empty but for a fear I feel
in case you wake up in my arms
and tear my need for your fierceness
back into your world

III

The heavy woman in my dream used the word
sacrilegious woke up the fear of a god I didn't
recognize back home the owl feather gathered dust
on the mantelpiece did I place it there to remind
myself of spirits in the bodies of soaring visitors
whose acrobatics stitch night to day with car
antennas and fenceposts leaving only our
analytical wasteland littered with scats filled
with bits of rodents and their minced skulls
and an occasional single feather as evidence
of omens never realized is it possible I've
brought my own superstitions to this island
on flights I never heard until a woman's voice
calls me out in my own dream but I'm confused
between memories of encounters with the white owl
starting with the night she brushed the windshield
after I lied to your husband about our love for each other
or when that one light appeared on the mountain road
outside the dreamworld telling us Stay or the time
I was alone on the island white truck out late white
owl laid out in the verge vanished overnight
and now this dream another mile marker where

all my beliefs fall off that shelf over the fire
the self in doubt the personal mythology
called into question the theft of a feather
what's the punishment in a land where another
older owl flies by day? whose feather was it?
two different languages both say Mine!

THE RAT'S TALE

What creature penetrates a macadamia nut? Pig? Mongoose? Worm? An opening has been made, similar to a finger hole one might see on a crudely crafted flute. Turning the mac nut shell—emptied by the unseen force or creature—I see scoring not unlike the cuts and nicks one sees radiating from woodcut images, from the myriad gouges and scoops that comprise the ink's destination—a belabored analogy, if I weren't trying to convey what must have been great and steadfast effort in opening up the nut, making enough of an aperture to enable the creature to extract the meat.

Where the meat once grew, there is now only interior wall curving and curving until emptiness itself spills out over the finely wrought orifice that no machine could make. The flesh is not here. Only the shell remains. The flesh is out there, moving through the undergrowth. It is change itself, teasing us out of our own protective tombs, our perfect pasts. The tree surrenders to the wind and so we fall, beating the ground, once, twice, rolling and rolling until that which has served us comes to rest in a disarray of debris where we lie like a jewel waiting to be found.

Put the empty shell to your lips just so, and make a long, penetrating sort of music which sings out, I am here! or Don't come any closer! But this shell's vibration tells only the story it can tell: the tenacious, gradual growth of the tree on the mountain. How many increments for the nut— hidden from the force or beast that dines on mac nut flesh—does it take to reach the branch? Put the empty shell next to your ear and the worm will enter your brain to tell you the rest of this story.

LISTENING FOR THE SONG OF THE THRUSH

I wake up exhausted and look for daylight
maybe the sun's still dragging its own fiery
countenance through night are we all
reluctant travelers in the dark Eternal?

maybe all this thinking wears me—
I was going to say *down* but I'm
already flat on my back perhaps this
is Limbo—I know I belong there
for that scene I threw last week

and other recent flirtations with Evil
doesn't Limbo include states of indecision
such as when a bed's warmth outweighs
the cool promise of a new day

well you know what they say
a pound of feathers still weighs
a pound I've reached the edge
again it's all this wakefulness
and resolution sickness I'm carrying

and bittersweet is this gut feeling
an antidote means simply dragging
my sorry countenance to the porcelain
where my greater self will decree

movement and thus begin again
would it really help to speak my mind
when all about are losing theirs? so
against the grain and yet here I am
with all the madness onstage

now flickering behind my eyes
or is that dawn come through
the branches? still no thrush
to claim first light still unwillingness

on my part to just leap off
this flat place this flat place
of pillows and dreams no
I'd rather wait for someone
living on instinct to call out

Wake up! someone who
doesn't live in her head
who easily abandons the perch
she claims each day at dusk

exhausted from flight only
to begin again her bright song

ISLAND CHAIN

Talk about rock fever what would you do
if you really couldn't leave if the internet
the dish and the telephones were *down*
what would you do if you looked down
upon that piece of sky called offshore
Hawai'i deceptively heavenly on calm
cloudless days no tug no floating barge
its two miles of chain slack beneath
the surface the usual illusions seen
from my house a thousand feet up
and until the gasoline runs out only
small fishing boats venturing north
on days free from buffeting trade winds
when the Kona winds blow from the south
what if the aforementioned barge-tug
arrangement not to mention larger
tankers even cruise ships that flicker
brightly like shopping malls at sea all
these visions that figure in concrete
practical ways into our island psyche
from toilet paper to tourists to my big
black tundra four door with vestigial
DVD player mounted in its ceiling
at a neck breaking angle what if they
didn't appear if the planes stopped
if the noise of the world we call
civilization diminished until all that
was left was the dot we call our island
adrift and quite free of its long chains

THE GREAT CRACK

—for Chris Leialoha's family and my friends Danny Guerpo & Keith Cabral

Down on hands and knees I lick kai pa'akai
salt from the sea my eyes working to see if
anyone's looking at me on all fours in my

primordial pose hands pressed against
the lava heart hovering near the edge
of the cliff behind me nothing green

to be seen not a shrub only grass clumps
gifts from birds in far clutches of rocks
at night goats cry this is a place that sings

the song called When You're Not Here and
when I'm not here the ocean never leaves
always arrives sometimes throws waves

down up here where the sun takes back
the water and leaves layers of salt like ice
in puka places I look over and see my

beloved friends twisting their knives
between the prized opihi and tumble
of wet boulders the tongue is my knife

one taste is all I need one long wet twist
between the white crystals and their home
high up in the pahoehoe of the Great Crack

THE DEWDROP WORLD

These days with the weather backwards
and the neighbor's stereo vibrating the walls
you wonder less and less about world peace
and look for meaning in small things
insignificant phenomena like snails
crossing the road in the dark before
rush hour or gatherings of mynah birds
outside Maverick's meat market
what are they talking about or maybe
as we move through the day upside down
and sideways we come away with ten hours'
worth of spiders web weaving and a sense
we're all in this together beneath the weather pattern
that's been on hold now for over a week
we don't like the possibility of tiny crab spiders
finding their way down our neck
inside our shirt but we stop and wonder
as we run our hands our fingertips
over our hair we look back at the corner
the square places and the round in our lives
the houses and hedgerows the webs
stretched over unlikely structures
bridging one world to the next
we bend closer listening to the creatures
spinning their stories into complex
geometrical patterns and where there's
intersections see the morning dew hold on
until the sun burns all this away

THE YELLOW LINE

Grass grows down it
down the center line of this place
green tufts sprout from the faded ochre stripe
that separates our comings and goings it's
stretched out between us a cautionary tale
unwound from Pololū Lookout
all the way down Akoni Pule
and the rest of the story
runs rings around our island

see how it clings to the black tarmac
by night shrinking by day expanding
cooling and warming up what we call
everyday existence as we rotate on our axis

you've seen no doubt the human nervous system
stretched out sans flesh and bones or strands
of DNA those spirals laid out 3-D
on the work surfaces of our imaginations
no table big enough
nor ether strong enough to keep us calm
as we consider how many times to the moon
and back the chemistry of information
will pierce us with its threads of phosphorous
hydrogen oxygen nitrogen carbon

well so it is with the yellow line
neither stop nor go this archetypal
agreement is older more primitive

pulled from the flames and mixed
with a little water for one long
one-handed daub

without end Amen
but not until the Ancient of Days
squints in paradise over the hinge
of his two-legged compass
the one that finds its way
into the hand of Newton
doubled over the art of stripe
as it travels over and percolates through
every pebble stone puka bump
lump serration aberration
in the jagged world of the diminutive
not a straightforward proposition

after all we see a yellow line
and say there it is but there it is
rather more than that
more along the lines
no pun intended
of the infinite
something we really
really relate to and
adopt wholeheartedly
if not egotistically

it is the yellow line after all
that petrifies us truly scares us silly
notice how we jerk back
when we inadvertently drift across
its profound illumination yes

it's the line we drew that frightens
holds its power over us
something inside us
non-negotiable

but you know having set out like this
on my side of the sweet yellow line
I think it's worth saying we need
a bit more of this sort of thing
wouldn't you agree? That is
the ability to agree
silently without getting
in each other's way

this arrangement of the yellow line
single or double so simple
such low maintenance
even when faded
the truth of it is there
if not a little annoying entropically
(how annoying the fading of the line)
if we can do so much with so little
why don't we do so much that needs doing
so little bit more?

STONES ARE CAPABLE OF THOUGHT

Keeping your place in a book on a windy day
a well-chosen stone comes to mind not to mention
marking the spot where you intend planting a tree
but it's inauspicious today there's a waiting period

and where there's time there's forgetfulness
out there in the middle of a field thus a stone
will speak to us when the moon's just right
and the tide will agree tumbling the cousins

of that stone in sheer rattling joy along the shores
of the world think of it the stone seems to say
as it tumbles in the lapidary ebb and flow of the sea
thoughts become smooth you see perfect for a pocket

where fingers now linger over a piece of green
Connemara marble whose veins too it seems run
thick with thoughts your eyes may widen my friend
as the idea lies petrified in your path something

you thought years ago suddenly there before you
in your way the choice is yours step over it
around it or pick it up and weigh it question its worth
wear it perhaps that's all the trend unless you decide

throw it and return to your glass house where
thoughts play out from room to room thrown
thwacked back and forth till they're quite beaten
subdued they make a clatter on the white tiles

of your days where they lie reminding you of
something you never said but perhaps should have
wars have been fought over less consider then
bending and picking up what was once served

saved beaten forgotten shaken from a shoe an
inconvenience in the middle of a long walk
a cause for pain in the sensitive realms where bone
and sinew ride close to the skin now with a warmth

in your fist you look and look at the object of your
preoccupations there in your palm and see
patterns spirals say or the face of a saint a depression
for the thumb a distant memory of boys and giants

shepherds and wolves the harder stories say
geological phenomenon of thinking in 3-D
the density the emptiness of the Buddha the seed
of invention the hunt the hunger the war the blood

all these things these thoughts now elliptical
trapped in orbit about your glorious imagination
till you close your fingers about around over the stone's
waiting and feel the transmission of its wondrous message

LOOKING OUT THE BACK DOOR

—for Cole Cornelius

What you have to understand
is that the beaten path at my
place leads to every fresh
start of something I already
left unfinished not really as
complicated as it sounds...that
door I call the back is actually
the front of my day and I want
to tell you as I'm on my way
to the toolbox tiptoeing over a
box of lawnmower parts here
and a disassembled carburetor
there maybe a trailer wheel on its
side maybe a tire iron right
where I left it like I say on my
way I catch the wind on my
face it's kind of in a hurry
and when I look to where it's headed
I notice a color I've never seen before
on a cloud against the mountain
outside my back door

HŌʻEA ROAD SHACKS

That decrepitude and corrosion and falling apart encountered when I first visited the Big Island has since become the charm of the place. Something in me needs to be tidy and well-advised before setting out each morning but I have learned, living 20 degrees north of the equator in this remote archipelago, that my sense of order doesn't allow for much truth-telling. History reduced to the black and white abstractions in a book doesn't cut it anymore. Tutu Pukui would say the same of her dictionary—what she's collected is a living force of expression not a geometrical arrangement for archivist's eyes alone. With that in mind, I set foot on Hōʻea Road some mornings and walk toward the ocean casting a loving eye to the patina of old weather-beaten tin roofs and tumble-down shacks. Looking up, I trust the wind writes all of this down.

OUT ON THE HEADLANDS

—for Steve Hedlund

Out on the headlands with one
eye on heaven's steep terrain
and both feet firm on the slopes
sweeping into Pololū that sacred
place that gave and took away
so much life a place of smooth
tumbling stones and sheltered woods
where casuarina stands sing
the song of the sea its endless
journey its eternal quest and we
ask forgiveness under these skies
under the world's weight of these
days mountains to sea our questions
are seven day's walking wide
and ready for anything the answers
following hard on a good day's
work we give we give without
looking back and take each
sunrise as the gift received

HORSES IN KOHALA

—for my neighbor Elizabeth Weidman

The thing is you are well-advised
to take a carrot in your pocket
for the long faces that greet you
at many a gate on the roads and
byways of this place Kohala
of the pandanus of the mountains
made smooth by time the dust
of heaven's stars fallen
a people who step on the long light
given us in free fall
Kohala of the two owls
one by day
and the high soaring hawk
who rides the ʻĀpaʻapaʻa wind
as if it were one thought
not the swirling and contrary force
that rules our lives—so
we have arrived here
in a place like no other
with a desire to reach out
touch these rolling hills
those velvet lips those
fierce all seeing eyes
there are those
who beat the air where
our hearts want to be

KEY TO NISHIMURA BAY

—for Rusty Cabral-Leialoha

The end of April can be full of surprises
take the key to Nishimura Bay for sunset
family and friends come to this rocky place
where the reef is luminous beneath the surface
moonlight writes itself on our heads
and the fire lingers in the wind well past
the cooking of meat the opening of beer
wine folding chairs eyes ears skin
we never guessed that we would see
whale breath rise like so many grandparents
breaking free of our ocean and its endless
tracks of currents farewell signatures
in the calm forgiveness of day's end
clouds ride the uplands of heaven
like proud sails hiding and revealing
Ka Hei-Hei O Nā Keiki or Orion
and countless other ancient lights
that guide navigators across infinity
we remember we are in this place
the fire is still sacred here
the one child who came arches his back
startles his aunty from cuddle to alert
and that is the key to Nishimura Bay
the one we left under a stone near the gate
so all of us might find our way to the fire
the one where our sweet lithe imagination
suddenly spills out of our arms ready to
plunge into the dust of Nishimura
but we breathe all this in and hold tight

ʻUPOLU AIRPORT ROAD PASTORAL

I've always liked the view despite the clouds
the telephone poles their sagging lines
playing slack key up and down the straight road
the way the northeast winds suggest each turn
of the languid mobius windmill blades

the way the cattle people this scene fretting
into each other's skins in these wide open spaces
or the egrets who rise up from their cross-eyed
meditations and hold steady their white
brush strokes against the lapis lazuli

the fierce channel where Maui heavily
weighs being an island against being
a mountain anyway what's in a name
that a search engine can't tell me
all I know is one foot in front of the other

and thoughts from forty years ago
looking to land—too much is never enough
we seem to say but now I wonder about
the mess we're in how separate we feel
just because we can pick up our feet

or take pictures with our iPhone
see that cow over there the one who
attacked the backhoe back when this was just
a field you know before the windmills came
that was a sight the cow charging the digger

defending her turf her patch of earth
she knew something we were slow to get
the winds of change and the roots
of technology running deep right here
in mid-Pacific where the whitecaps
hide the latest splash of a whale from us

'UPOLU AIRPORT DANCE

The runway of our small empty airport
at the northern edge of our mountainous island
is a grand place for a walk on the level
and at the turn of the year
a good site for spotting humpbacks
the strong trade winds press their invisible
hands against our backs like an old Irish blessing
until we reach the west end of the airstrip
where we turn around turn our faces
into that long steady ocean-crossing air current
my wife does a simple thing I won't forget
she holds aloft her black jacket by its sleeves
and runs with that contrary motion of the bee
making small twists and curls with her feet
she swoops and turns like a bird of prey
just out for a good time—in fact
I expect her to lift off the island
rise aloft with her makeshift parachute
and soar above the myriad wind-chopped waves
for lingering intimate joy among surfacing whales
who had after all been spouting all the while
not spouting you understand but blowing
blowing out before each abrupt fall of sea smoke
when their deep inhalations drink in everything
everything vital at the surface of the world
this is my wife's dance

LET'S LISTEN LONGER

An incredible coincidence
falls from the tree each night
and each morning waits
glowing in the grass

for our fingers this is
Easter and Christmas everyday
awake in a dispassionate
and curious way born

and born again skin seed fall
how did we get here after all
but through events that now
play reruns in our blood take

one acted out seven thousand
miles ago from here across two
oceans and one continent ah
but the ship's name was hindsight

and my own tongue the rudder
in the salty seas of analogy here now
pages of light where I point my dark
words twisting lines around the sun

till penumbra rhymes with rain and every
thing every living thing drinks and drinks
you call my name and my thirst is slaked
and bent like this my roof holds out its

wings spreading the downpour evenly
to the flower beds below hanging
fuchsia and strawberries Spanish
moss with its curtain flattering your eyes

as you look out on this scene gardenia
begonia Mexican sage Hawaiian tī
variegated banana and māmaki
palapalai ferns speaking in tongues

we list the ways we might
never have met let's listen longer
okay I'll get the wheel barrow and
meet you in the lower bed the mulch

too with a ten tine fork and old
newspapers old news we will lay out
on the ground ready to return
to the worms before sunset

DOUBLE TUBEROSE LEI

The trouble with that double
tuberose lei she said is how
heavy it feels I don't think
I'm ready to take on the
density of such scent and
bloom no take it he said
take it graciously because
it is cool and refreshing
like a morning rain that
blesses the work take it for
this day and the evening
too take it for love given
and renewed take the hundred
openings that have been tied
up and threaded through
with a careful love that will
endure long past the fading
hours take this lei this
double tuberose circle
of soft explosions
light up my life

YOUR NAME

In the cave of endless breath
your name finds its way to me
there at the opening there on
the threshold where I spend
my hours in hesitation I know
you're past hearing this but I'm
still afraid of the darkness
seems it doesn't matter that
you've reached out to me so
many times and all I can
come up with is one long
string of abstractions nothing
tangible for you to hold onto
I'm just trying to say out here
where the jobs are unfinished
small buildings I've started still
unclad in the rain and engine
parts still on the floor from
yesterday I'm just saying the
silence was hard for me I
kept spinning inside like a
tightening knot only one light
to come in and untie everything
your name finds me this way
and I can't even bring myself
to say I was waiting waiting

13 WAYS OF LOOKING AT MAUI

Over the rise on the mountain road
there in the clouds a line with wings
it can't be a cloud

Driving north a floating world
nestled in cumulus
and an ocean strewn with whitecaps

Everywhere I turn today you're there
how did a mountain move just now
you and a mountain everywhere

Leaning on the gate above Botelho's
that day the mower bucked down the fields
Maui was purple blue steel forbidden

Two weeks our friends stayed
every morning looking northwest at clouds
never really believing Maui was there hiding

When we first came here
it appeared suddenly and said
you're not alone

Those early days were confusing
Maui becoming Kohala in the north
or Hualālai in the south

The sun in a labyrinth
looks for a way out
Haleakalā

There was a time when giants got tired
and leaned on their elbows
cooling off in the ocean

What's the big deal a mountain is a mountain
an island is an island
Maui is Maui

Walking around on Maui
looking back at the Big Island
you have to watch out for the traffic

Hāna thickens the horizon
one day I found myself in Hāna
right away I knew I didn't belong

My friend Jack speaks of 'Ulupalakua
like an old lover
I better not go there

KEEP THINGS OPEN

We start our day early each with our list
you take yours down the coast in your fist
you call me saying Maui's unusually clear maybe
I should take my walk where I can see for myself

but I set about loading everything I pruned
one thing on my list leading to another
until a change in the weather reminds me
I'd better head makai to find Haleakalā

it's gigantic on the horizon a floating blue
mountain drawing all the sky's shadows down
to the dark bowl of the sea into that forbidding
channel called 'Alenuihāhā where clouds

shrink and fall laughing into whitecaps
but in a scientifically plausible reversal
night begins to inch its sapphire way
upward to heaven—connecting upper

to underworld with Maui's sleeping heart
beating against what's reasonable
I park in long cane grass and thread my
arms through a gate's galvanized frame

swung open—expecting and desiring
more than beauty can give me I
notice one fencepost leaning away from
the long barbed lines of wire nothing

48

standing still not even my joy not
on my list as it happens when a tractor
bucks down the field's hard-packed
edge toward me and I draw a circle

in the air signing Shut the Gate? but
the farmer smiles and shakes his head No
so I follow him out till I'm in my truck
—and I picture you returning home

your list a long road map of your day
your hand finding my own list still clean
on the kitchen counter where I imagine
your beauty smiles against what's reasonable

I TRUST THE QUIET

I trust the quiet only when I hear
your sleeping sounds your deeply
breathing form inhaling and letting
the night go free there in the dark
or when too the wind comes like a strong
verb pushing and shushing the trees
with names like casuarina and cedrus
and cocos nucifera outside our bedroom
windows then too when a single gecko
chuckles to himself or for our benefit
one of us dreaming the other listening
his laughter plays out from the ceiling
in comic comment the small voice
we were too busy to catch hold of all day
my heart also when I turn on my side
sends its semaphore message back in time
I hear my grandfathers snapping their matches
awake as I slip into the next and the next

LIFE IS A DREAM

After the earthquake that shook our house
by the neck and sent us outside where trees
danced unwillingly and their roots cast new
shadows with the sound of Earth's pahu
drums to the tenth power delivering distance
right to the front door and back again a
revelation how you and I serve wonder
before fear in the face of so full a deep
unknown orchestration and yes thanks
for pulling me into a clear place between
things that fall as you flew through the
doorway where I stood as if still back
in school but here we stood divested
of all that we own a long minute an overwhelming punctuation marked by broken
bottles of red wine and chimney stone
dust and shards on the green carpet—
Calderón's *La vida es sueño* the single
volume fallen from our bookshelves—
knickknacks stacks and picture frames
touched by that wind from beneath our
foundation October 15th 2006 fixed
the birthday of some unspeakable force
or being who visits at random and never
when you're ready for such demanding
guests and after they leave you breathe
the air anew but just in case complacency
sets in too fast the aftershock comes
and finally a sight one never sees a
languid owl leaving the now still trees

HĀWĪ SMOKESTACK

—for Gidget

One thing we know we have to do
is keep moving on when the stones
come tumbling down when houses
shift on their foundations we lift
ourselves up love the children more
take that long breath the world
gives away for free and forgive
the last person who crossed our path
with a little pain but the memory
of things that stood so firm and strong
landmarks that reminded us of home
such was Hāwī's smokestack with its
Kohala Sugar Mill stories the smoke
that will we know endure longer
than the stones which fell in
that October earthquake that
shook our lives to the core
and disappeared the day after

WATERFALL

This is what that first month of creation
must have been like in the days before days
were counted when it became clear that darkness
can never put out the light we're still in shock
but there's an irresistible radiance OVER HERE!
she's saying OVER HERE! how this waterfall
starts with one tear shed a drop fallen
from one eye make that two drops two eyes
soon water is spilling against the banks
dancing over boulders and deadfall alive
heading to the inevitable precipice of this moment
COME ON! she's saying I'm saying No way!
this is category 9 too much too fast too wild
but it's too late over we go what's up? what's down?
all is forgotten on that descent fingers splay
against the wet curtain I cannot see behind
I can't see anything one minute blinded
by her beauty the next both eyes drowning
Help! I can't even swim that well and so we fell
together in the morning light that is a memory
the two of us lying there on the wool carpet
a memory that blots out all memory if I let it
What day is it? Who's counting? I'm drunk
I had too much to think last night
and the night before So how did you two meet
someone asks Well the Himalayas come in here
Kathmandu parts of India Bavaria Paris Madrid
the little isle of Formentera London until we arrive
in a small town with a great tidal reach

marshlands malting barley alfalfa sugar beet
sailing boats called sharpies a North wind
so lazy it goes right through you big skies
and first sight of her a Cherokee woman
proud erect gliding through a gallery
wearing pieces of turquoise ocean on her wrist
and one strung through her ear with red coral
I remember a surge of happiness seeing such beauty
on the edge of the North Sea
flintstone buildings and a sea
with no mercy it was enough
just to be in the same place at the same time
this rush of stories and memories
a powerful cascade I know it takes awhile
to calm down as it searches out every secret
every gift given every kiss just like this
it's bigger than me this alchemy I had no idea
all these worlds coexist in the mist of this waterfall

SORRY FOR YOUR LOSS

Sorry for your loss people say and mean it
an old friend writes I hate that you lost her
and I want to say I'm the one who's lost

she's in plain sight everywhere at the post office
packages still arrive I'm walking in spirals
in and out of the house where straight lines

are anathema to her she of the curve of fullness
who imbues this emptiness with light and color
blossoms dancing in the mist of this new morning

I'm under the sea of a love so present its currents
pull me further and further out of myself
where is she? that is a question I've stopped asking

how could I have lost what I could never own
our love isn't like that never belonging
only a longing that began before I was born

she's reached the other side of the stream before me
this fast running flood tumbling into the sea
the mountain in shock trembling still knows

that's it no turning back or running uphill
unless we drift into the mythopoetic realm too far
looking and looking outside for something inside

all along all a longing she is the note still vibrating
ringing quietly on and on long after everyone else
got up and left no I'm the one who's lost

I know I've got to slow down I know running
in a panic before the sun sets before night
falls is useless she's been my compass

since the beginning and yes there were times
when the needle swung wildly around
or the pull of some magnetic force interfered

I am changed forever that's what's happened
grammar's inadequate punctuation pointless
how soft the hair on her head in that moment

when death entered how soft still the center
of this love I tell myself stop quibbling
okay okay my loss a loss I'll say it

I can't deny it any longer but really
a love this big's not possible to lose
a wave broke over my head all right

but I'm still in the canoe thirty days on
thirty nights I never fell out of bed once
all this reaching through dream state

I'll stop all this struggling eventually
learn how to breathe and swim at the same time
give thanks to everyone who found me
alive on this strange shore

I CAN TELL WHEN I'M LISTENING

I can tell when I'm listening in my dreams
cats push hard against my legs next morning
koi offer themselves up to the eyes open mouthed
the word *not* stands naked before the mirror

and that rooster she allowed to stay clears his throat
to say *Wake up! Wake up! She'll be here soon!*
my heart is sore on mornings like this aching
must have been some wild dance the night before—plates breaking

I'll be gluing shards together all the weeks to follow
still watching flowers bow their heads and fall apart
oh the ground isn't what it used to be these days
April showers blink and blink right through May

in their own way everyone understands moves closer
as if the earth's core has turned to water
opposites no longer attract get thrown out of orbit
vibration or tremor I can't tell the difference anymore

a crack in time has swallowed me up I'm wandering
in a place where the hallways never end
the front door stays locked the key hangs in a new place
at least my ears still ring that hasn't changed

sitting too close to the stage will do that but it's worth it
deaf or blind struck dumb for an entire month
her scent however is still alive her touch
let's just say I have a new companion

the old me had no idea no imagination
this version is pure not a speck of dust
gravity well believe it or not the rules have changed
I know now where the light grows in this listening

today today I just keep repeating that mantra
remembering is endless and oceanic
teach me the crawl quick I'm sinking with this breast stroke
a curious situation isn't it all this calm breaking

good thing she taught me to count the sets see the pattern
I can hear her voice telling me dive under
I never had a chance to remind her how much I trusted her
utterly and without bounds I can't shake the feeling

I still need her now that I have to stand on my own
others say you're not alone but this is different
leaning into the unknown asking her to come a little closer
so I can tell her all about it

NUMBER NINE POLE

I want to tell you about number nine pole
after Charlotte died I was about to say well
okay I'll just say it I'd walk my two miles up
and back on 'Upolu Airport Road turning

at the number nine telephone pole because
over the years I'd measured and timed and knew
from the double gates just above Botelho's
to the number nine pole is one mile but

shortly after she died I reached that place
and couldn't bring myself to look at that pole
because she died on the ninth of April
so for the last couple of months I kept walking

to eight or further to seven or even the main road
like Randall my dear brother and friend
with his seven league strides but lately lately
or should I say timely timely I see that pole

differently and so I stop now and dance
one hula at number nine pole I dance
in the slender shade offered at that time of day
between six and seven in the morning

first *Ke Anu O Waimea* singing *Ike au
i ka nani* "I see the beauty" singing *I ka poli
o ka ua e honihoni ana e* "In the heart
of the kissing rain" next day *Kaulana*

Hawi i Ka Hanohano because *Hoʻomanaʻo*
wau lā i ka hoa "I shall always recall
this dear friend" how wonderful this
turning I'm quite happy with this

there was a time when I considered writing
an ode to number nine pole there's nine
openings seven in the head alone nine gates
nine doors between each of us and the world

nine's a very special number there's nine
blessings for an absent friend so the light
goes out and in it comes again like a cat
like a melodious laughing thrush like

an orchid we sent to the shade house
only to discover a year later two or three
heads heavy with promise and each day
a blush deepening at each opening

COUNTING THE WAVES

—for Kai

Standing in the shallows near Zac holding
Kai finding ways to entertain the boy say
by kicking or splashing or ducking in to
come up sputtering and red-eyed a
curious thing came about when we
started counting the waves: the child
four months shy of two years took on a
master and commander disposition and
began pointing toward the oncoming waves
arm outstretched in an authoritative sort of
way making fierce shapes with his mouth his
lips forming for all intents and purposes each
waves' assignment in the steady roll call
of the tide a listing that threatened to quantify
the ocean and all its movement with a pull
as strong as the moon's ad infinitum
ONE! TWO! THREE! and SEV-EN!
most assuredly those two strident
syllables marking increase irreversible
until he shouted clearly TEN! with its
exclamation mark saluting the incremental
conquest of the turquoise shallows all the
way to the Prussian blue horizon when those
dreaded three-syllable approximations came
ELEVEN! SEVENTEEN! It's all over
Ocean the boy has you now the numbers
hold sway where fear once gulped and

gasped at the salty immensity of each
breaker despite one arm firmly founded
on the terra firma of dad's shoulder Ocean
your waves are truly numbered now

I LISTENED TO THE OCEAN

I'm going she said and broke softly
over my head while I just stood there
knee deep looking out watching the full
weight of meaning lift and sigh and I
just stood by listening until until until
she came back rose up and I tasted
a little fear on my tongue because she
rose high up but I stood there still I
felt a kind of trust flush through me
shoulders gut knees ready I was in the sea
and she broke hard over me pushed me
pulled me into her salty wet laughter
while I fell and splayed out laughing too
and then she left again

ONE GOOD EAR

One ear underwater I make my way to shore
sidestroke the way you taught me years ago
our younger daughter stays longer swims through
plumeria blossoms ti leaf lei and pua kenekeni
from the trees you planted still talking to you
still turning to say hey look at the mountains
snow on your birthday still talking to you saying
this is your day the day of your birth the shortest
day of the year winter solstice baby the earth
turning its body to the light again saying hey
now the nights get longer I love how you
came into this world on this turning

I've got my good ear beneath the surface now
making my way to shore how the sea
fills the chamber of my listening you
filling me up just as you rushed in through
my fingertips when I danced for you
the third night after you passed I'm
listening for your voice inside the waves
your laughter on the edge of whale song
you whispering is it possible you're so far away
and right here at the same time on the canoe
that took you they speak the language of sand
each grain a syllable each wave a new word

PUʻUWAI

I live in a place where the heart
is an upswelling where the air
is thick with ancestors all poets
luring me into the shadows
the heat of August passing even now
the year moving forward under
constellations whose arc also turns
I know I'm awake for it looking
for answers the wind avoids my
house entirely tonight will it
return if I stop asking questions
what is it about letting go that scares me
you should know I'm not alone in this
these days I look into a hundred faces
and see a thousand possibilities
here's the map it's not flat
that myth's been shattered
there's nothing to unfold
or read with the tip of the index finger
here and here it's time to begin
measuring from the belly button and
thinking about the source
but really it's also a time of gifts
and thus I have to stop acting
like people need to be paid back
stop paying out insults and jinxing
generosity that flows from a hundred hearts
what's given pulses in a thousand
ten thousand mornings I can't

count that high say in a million ways
say the stars or the sand or the tears
say the pores in the skin say the spiralling
breath between you and me all these things
that aren't things can't be quantified
belong to no department of human
resources no label here only the gut
the inside the upswelling about to break
open and cascade into the old ruts
this is true change and peace
this is the alchemy of the smile
the pollen beading up intimate
ready to be taken no one's looking
for thanks in moments like this
when the embrace is freely given
and limbs sink into each other
openly compassionately
time to stop putting a price on everything
that's a narrow existence
that's where death gets its reputation
down that cul-de-sac
when really it's more like
the dawn even now
I can hear the music
of that day of celebration
and I put my foot here
move my hips in a figure of eight
there's no turning back

IPU

—for Kumu Raylene Ha'alelea Kawaiae'a Lancaster

Her big gourd drum hits the ground in heartbeats through two layers of woven lau hala. The room becomes a big gourd in response and joins itself to our smaller head gourds so the heartbeats can pulse back and forth. Kumu appears cross-legged and full-bodied in one corner, a smiling volcano. Her hair forms the slopes. One hand takes hold of the place where the double gourd stays joined and the other slaps below while she drums the ground. Hand against gourd. Gourd against ground. Sound swallowed by the gourd in wrist-flicking slaps. Sound sent out in deep sonorous waves to our eardrums. Old and new at once.

Thirty legs at a time touch their feet to the floor, then pull quick brush-strokes in the air with their toes. Arms unfold full length following thirty hands reaching for a flower or the sky. Meanwhile the wind doesn't just blow outside it breaks over the roof and whistles its way through neglected windows. Whales' breath and surf blend out there in the approaching dark. Hands clap once in unison. Hips gyrate while the dancers advance, one step at a time.

Sexuality. The gourd. The long hair. The wind: ka makani: its fierce presence reminding us of an original indisputable power that can in a second become softer than any known touch. The wind—grandmother to the voice—leaves Kumu's lips and enters the dancers only to emerge in time as vocal responses to her rich, evocative chanting.

How would a quantum physicist see hula? There is nothing spectacular about the practice of hula—although some say there's a spiritual dimension—nothing extraordinary and probably not much room for the ego. More than 240 years have passed since Cook landed; since "impact."

67

Easy to consider the Western mind's acquisitive conquering nature in contrast to the Polynesian's "all one" sense of subtle interplay between origins and destiny. The Western mind likes to label things, say This is Nature, likes to separate us from each other. It likes to see walls built with our opposing thumbs, our voice boxes and our desire for permanence in the face of ceaseless change. Kumu exudes authority even when playfully remarking in gentle conversational tones, but she somehow jumps a dimension when she chants, becoming a go-between, a transmitter of stories, some of which were sung before impact. Many of the women listen to her with their eyes closed. Perhaps they are stepping aside from that acquisitive mindset, the one that answers the phone, the one that peels off the stamp for the credit card bill, writes a check.

Looking up from my journal I see cloud riders moving fast toward the magenta horizon. Now the group lines the walls. They slap their thighs by way of saying the arms are heavy about now, about an hour and a half into it. Women search out their water. Hips have circled; thighs strained. The sweat's on. Are we loosened up now? A male dancer picks up one of eight plumeria blossoms laid out in a row by a little girl on the edge of the matting which lines the wall and tucks it behind his left ear.

Monday night in the old coast guard station, a short walk from the birth site of King Kamehameha and a little ways further to the Moʻokini Heiau, a temple predating by more than 300 years the coronation of the man whose name gave us the word "king," Charlemagne; the man whose library comprised of four books made of animal skin and plant dye, none of which the great king could read.

Are there any questions about what we are supposed to be doing? Everyone laughs.

Kumu recommences calling up from her gut—no, somewhere, what is it about the human spirit? Somewhere from the green corridors of her own memory the wind breaks and spills itself against the outside walls. Know what's being given and what's being received, she says. Voice, touch, eye, word, tongue, inside again and again the same turns, moving, moving to a center from where one looks out in all directions, when one is at the still place, untouchable and yet most vulnerable, where the blood leaves its vision on the walls and small flashes show that light will find its way— Somewhere, what is it? gives rise. Kumu is a little girl studying how the waves move, later the manta with the light spilling, later a woman crying out in childbirth...

What started out as warmups and a chant that seemed to call upon whales to leap clear of the ocean's surface now forgets itself in a 30-strong akimbo of legs and arms. It's a wind-light-ocean dance that draws and draws through long umbilical windings that will suffocate us if we don't cut through, cut through till we are free once again inside our grand-mother's, grandmother's unconditional embrace. Only the stars under-stand this story as movement plays with darkness and light drawing and drawing along the womb-rippling tumble in waves, fierce and soft, wild and tame. Some call it "hula."

KUPUNA HULA

Last night the rain came in
lying there I knew that could have been us
the way we met: land cloud their heat
exchanging day for night *ka ua* is the rain
the rain found me out here this morning
out here in the pasture getting ready
to tell this story how we got this far
and step this way sweep one foot across
the threshold hold our arms out to each other
thus and thus we turn one side a hand flutters
close to the mouth we've come this far we say
we give ourselves now to something words
can't express we have to say this with the knot
they tied at birth circling circling we reach up
maybe clouds maybe stars in this story
the knees give a little our eyes beckon to each other
across the distance there's mountains now there's
a fierce hot stirring beneath our feet
but we shake our heads oh so lightly and smile
we've left ourselves at the door the windows
are all open everything's spinning or holding strong
we do this for each other
for our children
for the old ones

HALF A DOZEN REASONS FOR DANCING HULA

—for Aunty Ethel Yamamoto

I started dancing hula because one summer at the old courthouse in Kapaʻau, now the Senior Center, Aunty Ethel Yamamoto kept bugging me. "Why don't you dance?" We were sitting in the back corner on folding chairs, watching twenty or more people dance hula on the dark brown floor boards. I didn't know her name that first day. I thought she was kind of serious, maybe there in an official capacity, taking it all in. I just laughed. What I didn't know then is that Aunty Ethel's a bit of a party girl who's very capable of choosing her own moment to get up there and dance.

Sometimes the dancers used an empty building belonging to the Jodo Mission in Hāwī. We're sitting on a bench along one wall. This time she points into the group moving on the floor and says again, "Why don't you get up there and dance?" Then, with a wistful look into the distance she crosses her arms and says, "We need men." Well, yes, I can count the number of men dancers on one hand. But isn't dancing hula a girl thing? Maybe those three guys have been dancing since they were knee-high and they're crazy passionate for hula. Me, I have two left feet, I can assure you. Besides, I think I told her already, I'm here to watch my wife dance hula. Now, there's someone who's crazy passionate for hula.

I tell people I started dancing hula because I wanted to dance hula with my wife. Her passion for Hawaiʻi brought us here in 2001, and it took more than a decade for me to get up there and try it. Charlotte was pretty smart, though. When it came to off-the-radar stuff like your husband's going to learn how to dance hula, she never said to him, "No, that's not how you do it," because he would run the other direction as fast as he could. In my case, he'd walk the other direction, because he couldn't run far with those stagehand knees.

Most people are born head first. Learning how to dance hula, you're born feet first. So I hung at the outer limits of the dance area, put my hands on my hips and moved my feet. Easy, right? There's a sea of legs out there to follow, a few steps to the right, then the left, then the right, then the left, then the, what the? Touch some spot on the floor in front of you with your right foot, bring it back and do the same with your left, and then, what the? Reminded me of when I'm on my riding mower and the mynah's are trying to guess where I'm going to go next. They're running around jutting their beaks back and forth with their hands behind their backs like Groucho Marx, saying "What the? Where's he going now? Can't this guy mow in a straight line?"

For weeks and months I did the feet. I was not dancing hula. But you have to start somewhere, and without really thinking about it, I'd started. Without thinking! This was the key. Refraining from thinking is difficult for me, being a cerebral sort of person. I live in my head. A lot. (Doesn't mean you're smart) Now I had to live in my feet. When your head's in the clouds, your feet are far away, down there on the ground. Hey, are those my feet? Why won't they do as they're told? Who's in charge here, anyway? Aunty Ethel can do it. Uncle Kealoha can do it. Why can't I do it? Oh, I get it, those people were born that way. Like my wife. She was born to dance. That's one of the many things I loved about her. Me, I was born to think. That's just who I am. And this feet thing is really pissing me off. Don't talk to me right now! Stop showing me!

I think the bottom of the learning curve is a dark gulch full of mosquitoes and pig shadows with long tusks and there's no way I can get out because all the vines keep tripping me up and grabbing at my ankles. But then, one day, I see a light. Maybe it's a beautiful kukui tree. But it's the kumu and her ʻalakaʻi, and they're talking to me. She dances next to me and says, "Uncle Mike! Kaholo to the right. Kaholo to the left. Step point ʻuwehe. Step point ʻuwhehe. Kaʻo. Kaʻo." Wow, okay. If I can follow how she's doing it without falling over... Kaholo means travel. Oh yeah, Uncle Danny went holo holo. Now we get fish tonight! ʻUwehe means lift the heels while opening the knees. Kaʻo means sway. Kaʻo. Kaʻo. Just knowing the names of the steps is reassuring. But the most reassuring thing is knowing the kumu. Kumu hula means source of the knowledge of hula. One step at a time, I follow the kumu out of the gulch.

I'm dancing hula because of my teachers. I've met other teachers, powerful, charismatic kumus I respect and love, but at the time, I wasn't entertaining the idea that one day I would learn hula. I wasn't ready. Kumu Kaui and Michael came into my life at the perfect time, when I wanted to learn.

I'm dancing hula because I'm three score and five and I know learning to dance is good for me. I know the foundation of dance is rhythm. I just assumed some people have it and I don't. Discovering I could actually follow it? That was like discovering the moon always rises in the east, something else I waited until I was over 60 to find out. I noticed the waxing and waning, all right. I knew the moon played with the ebb and flow of the tides and tugged at the blood flow of women. Other than that, my knowledge of the moon's movements gets a little hazy, just like my knowledge of women. Sometimes 28 days in a month, sometimes 30, sometimes over there, sometimes over here. I'm like a mynah bird with my head spinning. What the? Where the? O mysterious moon, there you are. How beautiful. I think I'll write a poem.

I'm dancing hula because I'm finally getting out of my own head and touching the ground with my feet, to the beat. You know how many years I thought dancing was leaping around to crazy Irish music, with fiddles, flutes, uilleann pipes and goatskin bodhran? Skiddledy doo die doh die day. Man, I was free form, with the help of the Guinness, of course.

O mysterious dance! Okay Uncle Mike, we're gonna learn the hands. The mist. The eyelashes. The smell. The throat. The slippery ground. Watch out! Learning *Ka Ua O Nu'uanu* was a good first dance for me to learn start to finish, because each verse talks about one of the senses and that's what hula's about, expressing everything we see, hear, smell, taste, touch—Kumu Kaui adds a sixth sense—and feel. But move your hands and arms one way and your feet another? Once again, I'm an air head in an air sign learning to pay attention. I'm embarrassed. I'm uncoordinated. I'm totally lost.

Thankfully, there's repetition, there's a pattern, with the faithful, consistent beat of the music. Right, one, two, three; left, one, two, three. And, there's the faithful, consistent heartbeats of my teachers. I keep coming back to class because my two teachers, Kumu Kaui and Michael, her 'alaka'i, make it safe. I keep coming back because each of them has their own special style of mastery mixed with humor, humility and honesty. And yet, each teacher wields authority. They expect their haumana, their students, to fulfill their vision, dance by dance. I have only an inkling of my teachers' hula knowledge and creativity, but I see how generous they are with their precious time and respect them for it. They're both dedicated to their families, jobs and despite their very busy lives, both are genuinely dedicated to teaching three generations of students. This motivates me.

I am dancing hula because it keeps changing for me. Hula is not a fixed thing. Hula is fluid, like the ocean. Hula moves, like the signature of trees and plants in the wind. I'm not just talking about the three to four minutes of gestures and movements of choreography. I'm referring to the way of life that keeps hula alive. They say the sacred and profane hula dancing were separated out, back in the 19th century, but I feel the kumu reaches deeply into songs and stories, old and new, to create dances vibrant and alive. If hula stayed the same, if we got it in three easy lessons, would anyone continue? I can say, first the feet, then the hands. But it's not that simple. One day, Kealoha said to me, "Listen to the story." No matter how many times your wife or your teacher tells you listen to the story, you don't get it. Then one day, carefully enunciating his words, Kealoha says, "Listen to the story." Since he told me that, our small group of kāne has danced *Maka-kilo* in front of hundreds of people down at the Sheraton Keauhou for the Kupuna Hula Festival. Our own band played and sang behind us as we faced into the bright lights. When I heard "Kaulana," I reached my arms out full length at a right angle, without thinking. When I heard "Huli aku," I held one hand like a blade close to my chest and reached out with my other arm, before turning, and turning again. There's no thinking, as such. It's a listening like I've never experienced before. You don't get lost because the story guides you. And you know what to do as the story unfolds because you learned the choreography given by the kumu and you practiced, over and over. I know the principle behind rehearsal, having worked backstage in theatre for so many years, but never experienced its outcome like this, in performance. Also, paradoxically, you dance alone and together simultaneously. You look at your hands and stay alert to your hula brothers and sisters at the same time.

Then there's the kaona, the meaning of the story. When Charlotte and I visited Nu'uanu on O'ahu because we were learning the dance, the taxi driver waited while we explored the area around the overlook. The site is renowned for the way Kamehameha I forced hundreds of O'ahu warriors to their deaths over the pali. For me, it was hard to reconcile smiling and dancing vigorously through the song with this grim story in mind. But when we were up there looking out across the far reaches of the windward side, a thousand feet below, it started raining, and I understood we all have this long history of struggle that brings us to the present moment, that this history now mingles with the elements, that we need to be aware, that we need to bring our senses alive to the elements in this place, in this story. I don't even know if I have a right to this interpretation, but it helps me reconcile these things. It helps me understand that the dance brings the stories to life.

I am dancing hula, therefore, because I live in Hawai'i. Human settlement and conquest has moved across our planet to such an extent that much of our history feels broken, fragmented and incomplete. Here in Hawai'i we have a chance to learn about this place through the hula. Of course, this includes the language. Only the other day, Kealoha was saying if you take the word kanilehua apart, you won't find the famous mistlike rain of Hilo. The poetry of Hawai'i is a mingling of 'āina, 'ōlelo and hula and much else I'm unfamiliar with. I used to think, the last thing I'd ever want to be is one haole guy dancing hula up onstage, but I'm a human being in a certain place, looking out for the first time at the mountains, tasting the salt water along the shore, smelling the faint scent of lehua, touching the heavy morning dew this time of year with my fingers, hearing the shrill cry of a lone 'io above our place in Kohala, where the winds blow every which way.

DANCING OUT OF KOHALA

Dancing out of Kohala
thunder without rain
did that rumble come from Pololū?
did lightning flash inside
those dark stream beds
those hairpin turns
near Makapala?

Wake up Hala'ula!
Reach out Kapa'au!
We're dancing out of Kohala!

see the horses grazing at Honomaka'u?
Kumu Kaui remembers sweethearts
gazing on Maui from there

there's more kissing in the town of Hāwī
—say ha-vee like the vee in love—
under the banyans
kisses that linger
where movies used to play
in plantation days

look over your shoulder
passing Kāhei on the way
to Kokoiki where kupuna long ago
once hid the child king
stop in Mahukona where ocean
breaks history into little pieces
where ghosts play hide and seek

and the secrets of kupuna
rise up like flocks of birds set free

down the coast road now with our coolers
filled with leis and chicken wings
musubis cuttle fish salad all kine poke
you name it beers and hard stuff
win or lose all the way to Keauhou
kupuna following kupuna

we bring green
sing uluwehiwehi
and the land clings to our toenails
we bring blue
and a mist hides feathery lehua
a light scent of yellow ginger lei
like the first morning

we're still in shock from that thunder without rain
without our ʻĀpaʻapaʻa
the every which way wind
that runs through our hair
never mind
we've got Kohala anyway
or you could say Kohala's got us
mapped out in our smiles
on our foreheads
in the corners of our eyes

we're dancing these songs of Kohala
and we've got our costumes we've got
Kamehameha butterflies in our naʻau
but you know what? sometimes
the story doesn't end there

our lei flowers didn't make it
sometimes the story's never really finished
that thunder followed us you know
and the lightning came too

first came a kind of crazy dance offstage
when we were looking for answers
then we found our hula sisters
Nā Wai Puna o Kona
in a quiet place in Keauhou
held hands and calmed right down
while they sang in beautiful harmonies *he aliʻi*
Go they said
to Queen Liliʻuokalani's garden
and you will find your flowers
but we already found more than that
starting with those singing kupuna

the kaona of our story
the kaona of our song
thunder kupuna missing flowers
even lightning in dry stream beds
all makes a story inside a story
now we're dancing back to Kohala
with a story inside a story inside a story

this third story might be
all our stories in one big story
but there's no need to explain this to anyone
who's heard this kind of song before

HOKU MOON

In town last night for a meal after my three days away in Keauhou for the Kupuna Hula Festival to find the Hoku moon slipping through a net of power lines over Akoni Pule Highway rising up against all our earthbound rules defiant of our small visions even now I'm turning on more light to see my way remembering something as recent as last night!

Climbing a kou below her mother's Kava Bar with her little sister and grandfather on the ground I saw Kumu Hula Leia's older daughter perched like a cat people laughing and listening to music up the stairs—it's Friday night I realized—the night Leia usually comes to town. Across the street I pushed open the two-way screen doors of the Bamboo and found a corner where I could put my back to the screen near the kitchen door and because of my hearing thought the waitress said Oh you don't want to watch the waiter tonight? but later understood she'd meant John Keawe who was performing practically over my left shoulder but I didn't move I continued reading and remembering the kupuna hula while John talked about Kohala and kīhōʻalu style guitar and I did turn to see his wife Kumu Hula Hope and his two granddaughters dancing and whenever I bent to my food I could see faces focused on the glow of the Keawe family dancing and singing.

Did they know, these two kumus? Did they know what I knew about their hula sister Andrea? The same Andrea from their days with Kumu Hula Haʻalalea Kawaiaeʻa Lancaster; Andrea, now known as Kumu Hula Andrea Luchese, who participated as they did in ʻuniki under the guidance of Kumu Hula Keala Ching. Did they hear the news that Kumu Andrea's Halau Ka Piʻo O Ke Ānuenue won overall in this year's Kupuna Hula Festival?

What I love most about the moonrise that night is that it won't be caught in our net of understanding. How wonderful, two of those three kumus, lighting up the night in our small town with their gifts; their hula sister lighting up Kailua-Kona before heading back to her home in Ashland, Oregon. I can't pretend to know, but I'd like to think I can begin to understand the lineage in this dance.

YOU FLEW HOME UNDER A HOKU MOON

You flew home under a hoku moon
sometimes the moon looks like a star
without all the pizzazz comes down to earth
without all that jazz just steady as she
I don't know if it's falling exactly suspended's
what I'd say just hanging out quite a few
miles high I like to think she taught us
a perfect circle once a month don't hold
your breath she's back she's gone she
won't be long how do I know I've been
around she'll be back you like that song
I know you like that song and here she
comes you're thirty four thousand feet
she's got that beat a perfect orb she's
quite high and from what I understand
attached at the gravitational hip she's
locked into orbit forfeited her independence
before time before certainly I know you
were born it's historical kind of rhetorical
she's been around what can we do
just count her moods soon she'll be
waning no it's not what you think she's
gonna disappear a little bit each day

HOʻOMANA

Enlightenment! Every year here there's a parade
people bring gifts to a king who lived long ago
this time my hula brother Kalani falls off his horse

lightning struck me too recently but I didn't break
any bones concerned faces look familiar but I can't
shake this feeling I've just arrived I've stepped into

unknown territory something big's happened
and to prove it Kumu Keala arrives and without
further ado begins chanting he appears to be saying

whatever happens there's a song in it thanking
that moment onlookers might think Oh look
he's singing to a statue but that's the irony here

he's focused all right but not on anything frozen
or fixed Yes! blood was shed! loved ones! bones
broken grandmothers and grandfathers emptied out

like shells on the shoreline if we think too hard
this is where Kumu begins dancing he's paid his
respects announced his intentions now he shows

us the way—sweeps the air in great circles upgathers
the unseen moves forward taking quick steps birdlike
now steady balanced follows the rhythm kept

by the mute chorus of wahine striking their kalaʻau
it's an old language only one or two words get through
but it's essential this letting go of the familiar easy-going

banter like Have a nice day! or How's it going? I'm fine!
How are you? Whoever we were isn't up to the job
anymore we need to listen to what we don't understand

if we're going to learn anything some teachers make you
beg or worse wait cast iron statues are good at that but
there's an urgency and here is someone you can ask

and he'll turn up with a dozen ukuleles ready to teach you
beginning with yourself Here's the piko! Emptiness
where sound is born Here's the bones! pretty soon

you're strumming along it's not a trick but if that's
what you believe so be it subtlety or shock next thing
you're on the ground Enlightenment! my wife's death

struck me dumb but the shock opened my eyes and ears
Have a nice day! doesn't work anymore

FOR KUMU KEALA ON HIS BIRTHDAY

The poet walks through the world we don't always see
where rain runs red on the upper slopes
where the urge to strip off all the usual is so great
our grandmothers' grandmothers wake up
and start whispering under the stars

we're in water up to our necks
licking the salt from our lips one hand holding a mason jar
filled with precious rainwater from our neighborhood
another a green leaf
we get mixed up looking for answers

the poet says that's okay—he's even deeper
last seen where the cloth swirls around a whirlpool
onshore people keep checking the little windows
trying to see into that other world
look! he's on the sand shading his eyes

he's pulling words from his mouth
through a big smile crouching twirling
those who don't get it hide behind things
in case someone asks them why are you here
but there's an opening don't you see it?

he's saying he's chanting he's dancing
giving permission extending his fingertips
suddenly these aren't the words we left behind
on the shoreline beautiful to look at
but empty of life no these keep unfolding

emerging blossoming sending out
the intoxicating scent that crosses the planet
mountain to mountain cave to cave
secrets right out in the open listen
inside children's laughter

that's where you'll find him
a very serious place a fierce place
where the roots embrace
that's where you'll find him
rain imperceptible so soft it never falls

'ALALĀ DANCES FOR MAKANA

'Alalā swoops in stage left dancing on a layer
of air her form-fitting midnight black affair
sparkles every which way under those nine lights
high up over our heads we're all one for two hours
the bickering and tittering's suspended the world
continues to fall apart but she sweeps up all that
heaviness and beats it into nothing special
with her wings her smile well it's just as well
we're tied to the mast of civilization who knew
she'd be here working for singer guitarist Makana
the one who turns to the past for a way to be
here now all the way home I thought how
they're a good match released into the wild
as she was free to take a turn in the updrafts
of his higher octaves over the mountain road
riding right of the reflectors fast over ironwood debris
we'd heard the rain on the theatre roof now
I'm chasing the storm towards Maui stars over my shoulder
spinning every which way around the Kulu moon
lightning flashing like Haleakalā's on fire
a cloud signs its name with that illumination
music streams up from the center of the earth
and meets the soul no one owns this
go ahead take all the pictures you like
what we need from this life is free

TIME EXTENDS HER FOOT

October moving right along—if that's how it feels
then it's me right? needing to stop look listen
while Time crosses the street if she has feet
like that dancer performing *Hiʻilawe* within
a shout from Haleamaʻumaʻu Crater then I will
most decidedly no—correction—no decision
involved I will just plain well it's not
stopping I want or need it's more like Miller's
hummingbird poised and vibrating yes I'll
set my vibratory speed to an appreciative
flurry of feathers my neck hairs trembling
my eyes drinking and drinking while Time
overflows down my cheeks into my white
mustachio all the way to the cleft invisible
to all behind my chin hairs my Persian well
into which I have fallen the streets down here
run busy this time of year you have to study
the space between to get across maybe raise
two hands flutter your fingers like so and duck
behind the waterfall then hela right hela
left forget the white lines a gentle sway
of the hips will do what's out becomes in
all the moves somewhere between heart
and gut you know all that empty space
you call home put down the telephone
and the traffic disappears no need
for GPS you're only lost when hurrying
the sun can go down all it likes Time's
got her beautiful toes extended my god

you can fit the 'Alenuihāhā Channel
under her arch she's wearing black
you think it's a shadow or passing cloud
a sign of rough times ahead but it's theatre
a sensitivity to dark and light and audience
remember? audience? and color
how the long skirt of Time falls either side
of her long thigh lord I'm obsessed with this
am I going to be all right? it seems to help

HA'AHA'A

Yesterday was a good day for all sorts of reasons. Then, to top it off, my hula brother Kalani and I got up and danced at the Bamboo restaurant that evening. Mila (what an intoxicating musician!) played Waikaloa (the lighthouse on Maui, not the Hilton north of Kailua-Kona) and we made plenty people smile. Joan, the owner, called out Hana hou! and teased the roomful of diners now it was their turn. It was so much fun.

So this morning I was feeling pretty good about myself when I arrived at the Hawai'i Wildlife Sanctuary to dance with my hālau. Of course I talked up our Waikaloa moment from the night before. Pretty soon after the keiki performed and the wahine danced Mokihana Lullaby, we three kāne did what our hālau fondly calls the chicken dance. It's really called *Lei Moa'ulahiwa*, composed by Kuana Torres. Maybe with our Waimea blue shirts on we had a little kalij pheasant going for us. Still, we had our puffed up burlap ruffle cummerbund that we wore when we placed first at the competition in September. Kumu Kaui only had the rehearsal music, not the mele by itself, so we had to dance the whole competition version, the ka'i (entrance dance), the mele (song) itself, and the ho'i (departing dance). That was fine till we got to the ho'i. Brother Kealoha walked right off and disappeared behind a wall, leaving Kalani and me to figure out how things were supposed to go. I think we were so stunned at seeing our hula brother disappear like that, we couldn't even fake it (well, speaking for myself). We danced this way and that way and then we heard ha'ina! loud and clear coming from Michael our alaka'i, watching us from the audience, so we pulled it together sort of, and bumbled through the rest (again, speaking for myself).

What I noticed right away when we joined Kealahoa was that he said nothing and acted as if nothing out of the ordinary happened. I looked at Kalani and saw his expression, a kind of half-smile. Acknowledgement and acceptance with one look. Immediately I heard those three words in my mind, Let It Go.

I went over to the wahine where they stood watching Michael and two younger wahine dancing Keali'i Reichel's *No Luna* exquisitely. I slid my iPhone out of my pocket and began videoing their dance, thinking, Wow, maybe I'll finally get the hang of the second verse of this mele. It's not that I'm striving for perfection, just that I want to perform the dances with heart and soul, to convey the meaning through our movements, and really, to blend in with other dancers so I'm not sticking out like a sore thumb.

Or a sore loser! The thing is that being left there in front of the audience with Kalani was kind of a gift. My hula brothers and sisters always remind me, if you make a mistake, keep going! Kalani and I kept moving but I'm sure the expression on my face showed utter confusion and loss of direction. Did I say gift? Well, here you go! It's all yours! Your lesson in humility for today! Yeah that. That is actually a truly valuable gift, for which I am grateful. But more than that, acknowledging and accepting that I'm still learning and there is so much room for growth. Just last week, I saw Kumu Keala Ching doing the most sublime 'uwehe during his dancing of *Hi'ilawe*. It was like he took that split second and opened it up to reveal a whole world with that movement.

I'm in such a hurry sometimes I forget there's whole worlds inside our least movement, our slightest expression. If hula is teaching me anything, it's that I am my body, I'm not just in it, I am it. I want to live like that. You see great dancers like Kumu Keala moving so gracefully through the world. I saw the same grace with my mentors Jonathan and Moira, who were immersed in theatre. These artists engage fully their lives; they embrace reality so warmly it begins to vibrate and you can see into other worlds. Hula is life. Theatre is life. I love it. Can you hear that gentle cosmic laughter inside the Hawaiian word for humility, ha'aha'a? I can.

I LOOK AT THE MOON

I look at the moon and think of the world
my words will never touch up there
in the steadfast blue lunar reality seems
upended to the moving dot I call my mind
which begs me to hold up a thumb and compare

the cuticle I call my own with our
heavenly satellite its light never its own
as the sun plays with us no it's more
a piece of cloud laughing like Kohala's
mountains asking us to see through

an illusion that cannot possibly be
nothing everything conspires this way
into an impossible symbology of souls
meeting and colliding themselves
heavenly bodies with a soundtrack

that throws us somewhat we
check our watches note the location
establish a few reference points or
coordinates and breathe into our
curvature of make-believe

rest or stillness and soon enough
the half-moon becomes the top
of Buddha's curly head lifted so far
off the planet there's a quiet gasp
who said that how did we get here

and what's the point surely
I'm just a visitor here surely
I kept my promise and it's time
to move on surely the pages
will keep lifting and fluttering

in these ʻĀpaʻapaʻa gusts until
the story ends or begins or flips
to that really gripping scene where
we're ready to sacrifice everything
as if this world's worth saving

beneath the sounds of engines
belching and droning strangers'
voices inserting indistinct words
now the alarm's out and when the moon
disappears behind a rooftop
our blood runs wild

THE MOON

Always she
fullness to pendulous

When gone utterly: new

When slender as in her luminous blade
or heavenly bow: the huntress

Always ruler of the night
even in her absence

Before I knew better
I thought the sun followed her
in their round and round

When I began to know too much
she lit my way

After I suspected I knew nothing really
she lit my dreams
casting as they say
her pale as they say
silver coat across the nearest chair
wanton in her ageless way

I too never agreed with that first step
man's boot upon her face
its print still there

On nights when she tugs at the tides
if you squint you can make it out
a tear near one eye

KŪ KOLU

5th night of the lunar month

Standing under the canoe purchased from a resort
I wonder did this ceremonial waʻa
long enough for ten people to paddle for their lives
ever touch water
tonight I came for the music
a wild skillful pianist who plays boogie Rachmaninov
a cool sax player in shades
Ricardo on guitar
lead wearing a porkpie hat
and a drummer
well the subtleties and innuendoes were flying
and many were nodding their heads keeping time
I don't know what made me look up and study the rigging
a loose thread at the kanaka end
the stout screw eyes seated snug to the beams
lines taut bowline on the bite
kanaka and lupe a beautiful canoe
butterfly inlay lacquered thick
heavy as a tree
long as an unfinished song
three other occasions I stood beneath this waʻa
the celebration of my wife's life
kupuna hula rehearsals
and kanikapila moments like this one
this canoe stays suspended overhead tonight's no different
it's frozen in time
although that thin curve of light called Kū Kolu moon stirs my blood
I empty the rest of my red wine out on the ʻāina

consider it an offering or a blessing
I wish us well with our undertakings
I'm glad I came tonight
the news still warm on the home screen
I think to myself refugees aren't the problem it's refuge
a place to do what the piano player said
cross that emptiness between each of us for songs of love and loss
letting go or hanging on burning up or freezing
moving on or staying behind
I leave early
head out beneath that long curved moon
that blade that opened up the night
I walk out while the songs are still fresh
half full or half empty they say
I say the music rises under that waʻa
keeps us afloat
not just up here defying gravity
but moving out there
island to island
looking for new shorelines
and answers to this restlessness
some of us call home

'OLE KŪ KAHI

Seventh and twenty-first days of the lunar month

There's two groups of 'Ole moons, waxing and waning either side of the full moons (in Hawaiian culture there's four full moons: Hua, Akua, Hoku and Māhealani). 'Ole, you may already know, means "nothing," as in A'ole, something you hear parents say a lot... For the kahuna, who otherwise worked with each particular moon in mind, the 'ole moons were apparently "days off," no need to do anything...the 'ole moons are typically considered "unproductive" for planting or fishing. But the tenth night's moon, 'Olepau, marks the beginning of a planting phase..."pau," you might recall, means "finished, done." There's the 'ole winds to consider as well...when everything's still...I find it remarkable how in-tune the calendar is to this day...even if it seems at odds with the actual weather pattern, the narrative that goes with the Hawaiian moon calendar in its various interpretations, depending on which island and/or which family, is chock-full of very interesting detail. When the wiliwili tree is in bloom, it's shark mating season and that's when they will bite. In these poems named after Hawaiian moons, I am merely associating events in my life with phases of the moon occurring at the time. My intention is not to explain the moon or any of its names.

Nothing prepared him for the problem
that grew beneath his smile
a small stone caught in the throat
an ossification
secretions of notions he couldn't swallow
whole phrases in lost languages of the heart the gut
stuck sentiments he couldn't cough up
hardening layer by layer
where resistance hadn't earned its name in his litany of hours

so he was surprised when the surgeon
her long black dress open at the knee
dancing over his chest
twisted the arc of truth open in the air
until the light came in
shining blinding

after the ordeal
he unfurled his fingers from her hair
his eyes dimmed
exhausted wet
a sense of loss as he peered at the thing he'd allowed to grow
its bundle of hardened fragments mountain scree
shoreline coral
childhood hazelnut
island kukui
all pulverized and pressed together
gold flecks reflecting what was left of an ancient promise
arousing that old pang of remorse
an Irish nurse came in offering *uisce*
but he thought she'd said whiskey
and shook his head
wai she said
agua
and beneath his smile
the waterfall made its thundering way to the churning pool
where he stripped and followed

ʻOLE KŪ LUA

Eighth day of the lunar month

Three nights of Perseid showers came and went
their lights flirting with the atmosphere so well
I missed them entirely
either slept through those first dark hours
or squinted into moonlight
that spilled and stained cloud cover
then I threw off my own bed cover before dawn on Sunday
and silently put more than I needed in the car
headed down to the shore at Kapaʻa
arriving in the sweet light of island dawn
my hula brothers and sisters there before me
a fire blazing in the stone pit
a fire you could see from Hāna across the channel
I'm sure our own inner fires lit up the distances since three A.M.
we're wearing the colors and symbols of hula and Kohala
our fern-printed muslin too
photographs taken later document joy on our faces
but this is a special journey of joy with gifts for Kauaʻi
across the water to our west
the places we'll be dancing about
but before we break our fasts we assemble above the coral beach
where an owl flies close
right over our heads
and on into the woods towards Māhukona
only then did we release hoʻokupu
our gifts wrapped in kī
given to the ocean's soft tugging embrace
we faced west

I'm not alone imagining everything we did that morning
made its way to the island of Kauaʻi so many miles away
Kealoha chanted strongly at sunrise
and in the circle his voice was joined by Alakaʻi hula Michael
these are the moments when the name Elderly Recreation transforms
elevated by ritual and protocol
and I confess when I saw my solo kāne offering
swirl inside the shoreline rocks as if reluctant to go deeper and further
I felt here's the truth
here's the visible world telling me
showing me
let go
be out of control
so I gave my thoughts away also
my dance would celebrate the island of Kauaʻi
Waiʻaleʻale Hanalei Kekaha and the kinship coastline nearest Niʻihau
you'd have to be a big winged bird to make that trip in one song
hula's done that for me
transformed the literal into both personal and universal
mountains so steep they reach far over my head
inner landscapes so vast and varied
you'd have to be an ʻiwa bird to make it
ah but why get all dramatic
I'll just reach through these twinges and aches
for the small shells twist around
turn back for the beautiful little berries so rare
wear that lei
be the dancer this late in the day
it's okay
if hula celebrates Hawaiʻi then it's a two-way gift
after we dance our five dances
we convene in the pavilion
sing our blessing by the food

we look out
see spinner dolphin pods just offshore
if the owl is that singular master of moving through uncertainty
and transformation
here are the ocean's dancers rising and gliding together
I can hear it in our voices
ah look oh my oh that's beautiful yes
the sun rises over the mountains we call our island
shines on the glistening body of one spinner
rising clear and free of the surface
ooh
and then as my wife liked to say
good things come in threes
a rainbow appears arching vividly between cloud and sea
bridging seen and unseen
a flourishing signature written on our huakaʻi
our journey in learning
as if to say yes
you're going the right way

ʻOLE PAU

Tenth night of the lunar month

This distance between us is growing
this first day of August clearly saying
Here I am
look around
just let yesterday try pushing past me with its just one more thought
let's let balance correct itself again
and again
let the single spider dangle
between arica palm legs and spray of purple vitex
can you see it
beneath that strand of silk
Haleakalā smiles wearing a lei of slow moving clouds
we're all in suspense over the season my ancestors called Beltane
fun as it was watching all those hot-blooded young women
leaping around the tent on the mountain
next day I cultivated half a dozen lavenders
the smell of peace still on my fingertips
this tenth night of the first waxing lunar phase called Anahulu Hoʻonui
starting with the new or Hilo moon
ending with the ʻOlepau moon whispers now's the time
for planting ulu eggplant or string beans
I guess that dance band planted some seeds in me at the right time
movement is good
what's not moving I ask you
the time for planting sadness with its scent of dust is past
besides this isn't just another orbit marking time in space
if we're going to grow up and flower
then we need to be students of movement

103

swell break open emerge
forget the madness we call our busy lives
the twisting and blinking between blossom and wilting
though we may grumble about the mess
I made one three days ago
I pruned the old lime tree
I threw all the dead branches into the gulch

MŌHALU

12th night of the lunar month
—for Michael Regan

Two men in the dying light
the round table spread out
raw fish kimchee cucumber red pepper paté seeded baguette slices
one sips Argentinian Malbec the other beer brewed not far
when they can't see they begin feeling amidst the small plates
fingertips brush against wasabi into shoyu
looking for the opener
till they pick up the table and everything on it
move into the moonlight where secrets will be revealed
the single life waxes one
it's simple uncluttered
and anyway could I live with anyone
could anyone live with me
by now the cats become mere shadows on the stones
we're talking about death
encountering the finality of a loved one a wife a mother
we talk about embrace embracing embraced
all the variations on holding out your arms
to your neighborhood your hula hālau the wind
change planting dancing
stories names places dates distance years time
it's been awhile since we did this
and it's getting darker
some people call it catching up
our angular positions soften in the chairs
our moonlit faces leave our bodies
and rise into the night

down below our arms are outstretched
hands ready to receive those illuminations of our days
that didn't spill into the deep
regardless of the endless inevitability
until that scent of finality brings us back to clocks and calendars
and we clear the table
bring everything we didn't consume inside
and walk to the car that will take one of us home
the other already home
moving soon enough along invisible walls
searching out undefined doorways
fingertips wide awake still talking

MĀHEALANI

16th day of the lunar month

The day the white-eyes come the little mejiro
hop-flick their way branch to branch outside my window
searching the leaves intent on winkling out larvae
oblivious to my gaze
my wide-eyed hunger for moments like this
lured by beauty even when she wears eye-rings and olive green
she stands still for one provocative beat
vibration holds its breath I hold mine too
as I study first-hand the outlaw plumage
and hint of Sumi-e circles 'round each eye
everyone's hungry on this planet
I'm eating seasonal appearances of little passerines
and they're eating little bugs or sucking nectar
there's gut-ache and heartburn ahead for all or one of us
because there's too many of us because there's not enough
neither 'amakihi nor precious 'akepa can keep up
because when we're not looking
mejiro invade Hawaiian forests
where the island honeycreepers have been pushed
the truth of the falling leaf spiraling to earth
is written in a language spoken when every living thing
was still speaking to each other
nothing fell off the cycle of life without a smile
loss didn't tighten the lips or furrow the brow
breathing in was a song of praise over breakfast
breathing out a piercing ululation that fed the world
now a hawk soars out of the forest an i'o
now we're the ones outside the windows

turning and turning necks to their limits
our eyes search and feast on this morning's cloudless sky
glide past the last full moon as it falls past the roofline
the long edge of blindness where three gold-dust day geckos
inch towards each other flicking their tongues into the rising sun

LA'AU PAU

Twentieth day of the lunar month

Moving towards that place in the ocean
where the moon seems to spill its light
seatbelt tight against my left shoulder over the washboard road
I can't go any further
the cliffs of 'Upolu held me up once before here on the edge
where dreams trade places with everyday walking life
now I see if the moon can do it I can let go too
but if I'm honest I'll tell you
fear dances a merry dance at the roots of my hair
don't ask me what's to be afraid of
I'm just being honest I guess
anyone can dance that dance it comes with mortality
I feel this gentle lift from the northeast
I'll take gentle today I know how the wind can blow
if she lets go no I'll do the letting go right now
out of the truck toward the sound of surf
relinquished by the setting moon
sloshing hushing
boomphing against the broken limits of land
sun rising at my back Maui mysterious above thick band of cloud
deceptively linear from this distance less than 30 miles
and we think straight lines are a fact
at my age I've stopped believing in straight lines
my older daughter tells me write about nothing dad
write about nothing to write about
because everything happens in the nothing inside that nothing
so I come to the edge looking for the light
missing from last night's moon

my head's spinning with full moons
moons before moons after this emptiness
new dark moons circling through my calendar pages
it's enough this nothing
listening to it I sense its power
hear its hum coming from the ocean floor
feel its movement coming for me through long grasses branches
its dendritic reach intimate with mine
no wonder fear dances at the roots
it can't go any deeper
there's no discussion here
just one long embrace

LONO

28th day of the lunar month

Last night my usual confusion around
Hawaiian pronunciation and meaning
resolved when Mila joined us after his set
at the Bamboo restaurant and explained
as he pinched his tears away his take
on *Ka Ipo Lei Manu* a love poem written
by Queen Kapiʻolani for her husband
David Kalākaua in the late 19th century
when the king was in San Francisco
but when his ship returned
draped in black the flags halfmast
the queen's poem of love transformed
into a song of mourning in this mele
that I heard sung by so many I heard
the word *manu* which can mean bird
and saw in my mind's eye the ʻiwa
which I thought I heard in the third
verse the black streamlined thief
the frigate bird the one who soars
inland ahead of storms I thought too
of the iwi the bones the bones we felt
chilled earlier when Mila sang falsetto
but no I was mistaken it is the little
iʻiwi not one of the rare red creatures
we've come to love in photos taken
by Jack Jeffrey no it is the young bird
pōlena i ka ua
yellow in the rain

as if my misunderstanding led me
to the hidden meaning of this song
ke kaona o ke mele
the queen thought there would be more
and hearing Mila say this I cried again
realizing I'm not finished either
this morning I'm still walking in the rain
wishing I'd paid attention when
but when is a moveable feast
and hungry as I was I hesitated then
and now this misty morning two 'iwa birds
sail out of the confusion
over the windmills at 'Upolu
they soar between two arms
of a storm feeling its way
along Maui's slopes and shores
to our side of the channel in Kohala
where I wonder does the 'iwa bird
ever stand still my runaway mind
jealous of those hollow bones
that streamlined form
I get drenched by the storm's
embrace strip off at my truck
this is what stopping looks like
an empty day on the calendar
a butterfly opening its wings on my wristwatch
I'm remembering other times alone
long ago moments when I stopped
and boiled rice swam naked thought
there would always be time
I live in a place still grieving
for a dead king and what's left
of the i'iwi birds so we follow

the uplands curving our beaks
toward the nectar
like yesterday's right here
there's no metaphor for stopping
even a rock moves its molecules slo-mo
allows itself to sink beneath the surface
stop is a verb curled up under the hau tree
healing itself minding its own unfinished business
asking what does this song really mean?

THE MAN FROM RIGA

Some context. Back in the seventies, and before we were married, my wife came to see me at the Royal Opera House, Covent Garden, in London, where I was working as a stagehand. "The Garden," as we called it, was home to both the Royal Opera and the Royal Ballet. The tall dock doors were wide open and Charlotte simply walked upstairs from Maiden Lane to join our small group standing just offstage. Onstage a male dancer was performing grand jetés around an older man center stage with one foot on a chair, one arm draped with what appeared to be a Burberry raincoat. Charlotte couldn't take her eyes of this scene and started batting my arm with the back of her hand. Who IS that? she said. I leaned towards her and said, That's one of the most famous choreographers alive today, Sir Frederick Ashton. No, no, no! she said. The dancer! Oh, that's Baryshnikov, I said. He's recently defected from Russia. The stage was utterly bare, except for one chair in the center supporting the old man, and, dancing impossibly magnificent circles around him, the young Baryshnikov. Well, I say young, he was the same age as us. More than thirty years later, the great dancer came to a theatre near us in Hawai'i.

Tonight I'm awake near midnight with images from the Kahilu Theatre's presentation of Baryshnikov and Laguna. A bare stage. Marvelously refreshing—to me—hangings, that is, the "blacks," or drapery making up the borders and wings. For one thing, no lights were in view from the seats; none of the lighting suspended from the flying system was visible, only the effect of lighting seen indirectly by the audience. There were several tall standards facing the audience from upstage, but I'm not talking about these, which I consider part of the set and not the same as incidental lighting. I hope that makes sense. Let's just say it's refreshing to find the lights intended to illuminate the performers weren't blinding the audience. I seem to be the only one who cares because I've never heard anyone complain about the Kahilu's usual modus operandi.

Is all that an important component of the remarkable performances we witnessed tonight? Oh yes. The proscenium arch and its contained field of stage, drapery, lighting and props, areas of entrance and exit, were simply left alone to do their job: provide a theatrical context which allowed us to focus on the performance and not be distracted, for example, by badly hung wing drapery that does not meet the stage but rather presents us with a distracting break or breach in the suspension of our disbelief. Too often at the Kahilu we have seen the legs of the stage management or lingering performers walking around backstage during a performance.

That said, all that remains is the bare minimum—just as well, with an ambitious international tour by a dancer as famed as our man from Riga. I mean that bit about fame. Nijinsky, Nureyev and Baryshnikov, in that order, wouldn't you say? At least in the popular imagination—at least in my imagination—I shouldn't really speak for anyone but myself (but judging by the spontaneous and rather fulsome round of applause given when Mikhail Nikolaevitch Baryshnikov simply walked to center stage at the outset, I am not alone (Ana Laguna received no such welcome when she made her first appearance).

And not to belabor the fame bit, but the very warm and immediate standing ovation two hours later—well, I did recognize a couple of neighbors who were slow to rise, if not on principle of countering the crass tendency of late to give standing ovations far too easily, than from sheer effort of hefting their bulk from their seats in Row C—as I was saying, the standing ovation in this instance seemed to me to be an immediate and heartfelt appreciation for magnificent artistry given not just for one performance but for one lifetime, for a precious glimpse of that artistry at any given time in the past four decades, artistry which inspires us, gives us hope and an old fashioned though much needed sense of exultation, vicarious though it may be, just knowing we truly are nearer the angels...

But—a very big breath taken here for the exquisite irony of what I am about to say—this was a performance that held up our mortality like no other.

For all the reasons—as if we needed to have it spelled out—of fame, artistry, time, and age, tonight we saw ourselves, our infant curiosity, our adolescent immortality, our ages of innocence and experience, drunk with one finger to our lips at one point, looking for something under the carpet again and again, dancing on the table with our arms around each other, gently head-butting our partner's chest, wiping the floor with our skirt, scratching our ass, and touching the inside of a curiously abandoned shoe as if that gesture alone will bring back lost love...

...all bound up with life's flight come to land after all. Sweet gravity! We all can relate to sweet gravity! I should qualify that. Those of us who know age 60 plus intimately can certainly relate to the care needed in descending from the table top to the floor; to the gentle, intimate suggestion of elevation in the arms of the beloved; to the grounded nature of our movements, our expressions, our language of physiology—the universal language of dance which rippled through the audience mighty like a squatting Kali with her tongue out fiercely and eyes wild, like rage, frustration, routine, like fleetingly putting our hands in someone else's pockets, or blissful, gliding joy.

A heaviness, my wife said.

Selfishly, I thought Baryshnikov and Ana Laguna danced for our generation tonight. We're not dead yet! There is a fierce, graceful way for us to proceed. We can all agree to be at least somewhat more aware, somewhat more conscious of our position in the universe.

As usual, I have misgivings about these sorts of generalizations and I immediately cast a net of doubt over everything I've just said. After all, the little voice over my left shoulder says, It was a bare stage. Indeed, the props were symbols of domesticity, human life, and as such, vehicles for play-acting in isolation. That is to say, in a world without nature.

And yet, that is not the scope of the exercise, unless one sees our relationship with or in nature as "existence." We are indeed social creatures. We are indeed bound up in relationship from the moment we're born. And in the case of a performer of Baryshnikov's stature, the relationship of one to the many engenders an extraordinary and overwhelming demand to keep on rising beyond the human sphere. This performer has chosen an honest relationship with gravity itself and by so doing has shown us a way to embrace our mortality in increments of grace and intimacy. And if that sounds too much like a spin on baby boomers coming to terms with age and all the slings and arrows therein, I do recall the time the dancer lay on his side under the table with his back to the audience, chest heaving while he caught his breath. That sense of pace and inevitability was as much a part of the performance as Ana Laguna's stunning ability to move in ways that reached inside our guts and brought tears to our eyes.

THE DANCE OF DISTRACTIONS

—dedicated to the Courtyard Café at Nanbu in Kapaʻau

Molecules
between you and me
don't care about
prepositions
but they do mind
noise
they steer us away
or close

grammar is dead
it's attraction
or repulsion
either way we shall shun endings
and embrace apostrophes with alacrity

it's the end of privacy
who wants it?
death is quite private
birth less so
life a cacophony

would you like two
sugars
or may I suggest agave syrup
no thorns no
just the sweetness
there's the phone
there's the clatter
of Carol's plastic dishware

inherited from Susan
who now administers
her son's plumbing business

he wants me to call
because my spud gaskets have arrived
will the act of refitting
those gaskets
gaskets we want gaskets
make the singing toilet
keep its mouth shut
automatically of course
it used to shudder
not the lid
the pipes

is lost
just wandering with distractions?
if wandering
is a walking meditation
until sunset
then getting lost appears
and scares the bejeezus out of you

when are distractions inspirational
just there in the

don't pull that thread!
the whole thing will only get worse
see how the tea bag
tucks its tail inside
the ceramic cups Carol brought
all the way from San Francisco

some voices so strident
it's inescapable
their power of distraction
proving whatever you can do
to a cloud of distraction
is after all
a preposition
between you and her

MGAMBO: HUA WELEWEKA

We can say oh the color the touch how
unusual exotic how nature came up with
autumn in red velvet wearing her grey
down-covered pearls as November fades

we can say these things as she curls
and opens this child born under Scorpio
ready to melt at your fingertips until
you learn she's tougher than you think

not only will she return she'll come
'round again and she'll come alone
sure of herself knowing she will
stand out that the young men will

surround her refresh her drink grow
pink with envy as the old boys elbow
them aside for the elusive prize but
she will play them they will never

see her antique skin in the morning
she'll be long gone all that remains
less memory than perplexity
explaining exactly what was said

who danced with whom when the bells
sounded toasts raised only we are left
with the center of we can't put our finger
on it something beautiful and still here

ON SEEING JULIA'S WORK IN PROGRESS

Up on Beers Road the artist wakes up each
morning rising from bunched and wrinkled
dreams and walks out before someone
she thinks she knows too well can catch up

this is how she finds the light behind
the ordinary the way shadows tell time
what to do as they move over the ground
we see her crouching here hand reaching

touching the surface of things the many
things the plane of passing glances
offers to the trained eye her repertoire
flickers busily we could say interacts

her inner world briskly works
against the outer trees leaves
bark stones pebbles dust branches
alive and dead some semblance of order

but little recognizably formally human
we could say that's not what she's about
color being her language tempting to say
solitary tongue with whom can she dialogue

after all when it comes to color? she
stands here and looks about. Huntress.

A SHADOW

A shadow turns out to be a boar whose one grunt
lifts him slightly lifts his whole muscular body
before disappearing my eyes grow heavy
just remembering this moment just feeling
the exhaustion of weeks traveling to reach home
arriving here where all the question and answer sessions
play out in my sinews collapse into each other all
their color overlay overlay overlay in a tumble till
they're one bristling ridge-backed shadow startled
awake crumbs of soil falling from a long snout
innocent devastation of wildness discovered
in the garden what is a garden I ask this morning
that excludes wildness meanwhile the search for balance
resumes we find tracks punched in the wet soil
the turf easily pushed aside twisted out of its
green illusion of calm expanse after months of rain
and the twelve foot farm gate pushed open we imagine
a powerful shadow breaking free bearing hard head down
shoulder against metal in a mighty bid
for the undergrowth where the only rule is survival

THE WORK OF HUNTERS

—For Chuck Ferreira

The work of hunters is never done they like to think
and thinking's never ending with their pursuits in mind
even older ones now reduced to staying home
weeding their small patch of greens
ones who see change from a long way off
maybe pre-plantation days maybe ancient
family understandings and ways to read the signs
all creatures having their respective languages
roads they travel habits that can't be broken
habits that surprise us when they shift their
patterns the way pigs will fool you coming
at dawn one morning and dusk the next day
midst full moon one night or the rising of it
the next even a thin curved smile of a moon
some say will bring what's called the game
where do they sleep?
oh that will change with these nomadic types
where eat? well just look next time
and see how well they turn the soil
where it's good and wet
they're not after your prized roots
but those might pay
for a night of hunting worms
the hunter and the hunted changing roles you see
and here's an idle question why is it
we call hunters on the land by that name
but on the sea or shore it's fishermen
can you tell me that?

aren't they hunting
with their nets, spears, hooks and depth
finders, their maps on paper and too
those maps we can't see
like all hunters' stories told and held
in the country of their minds where
it's so dark only the faint constellations
of their grandfather's words can guide them

HE MOVES EARTH

—for Norman Sakai

He moves earth
to shape subterranean places
for holding the people's past

how the people squat and release
the wasted once wanted the refuse

once accepted into dark places
beneath ground we walk on everyday
not thinking till we fall through

and too he shapes earth for
the foundation levels the field
evens the surfaces

makes perfect the mold
to hold concrete
what was once thick liquid

now hard and fast held
holding frame roof and all
the emptiness we call windows

doors rooms he scoops
molds and folds for the berm
where the rich man withdraws

with his bigger emptiness
hiding from the wind
berm ditch gulch

nothing too sacred
we call the earth
soil and he moves

and scrapes
wears his cap to one side
speaks sparingly

LIFEGUARD

—for Danny Guerpo

He sits on high
scans where sea
and sky join sees
the boy too small
for shore-break
the father too far
too unsure himself

this morning he
rescued a broker
carried away
on the rip tide
by lunch time
the pretty girls
all in a row

glistened over
a sea of towels
he sees everything
with confidence
and caution moves
through whitecaps
and swells catches

rhythms rides
the power expects
nothing back for
all the respect he

pays ocean and sun-
worshipper alike
but at the end

of his day when
he drives down
the coast road
in his old truck
boards in back
he wonders who
would save him

ICARUS INVENTS SURFING

Icarus was the one who invented surfing
feathers clenched in each fist if his father
was the father of lofty observation then
the son descended into a watery heaven
leaving the middle path forever one arm
waving free and a profound immediate
understanding of surface tension look
what happens when you don't do your
homework drifting around places with
exotic names ready to drop everything
to follow the waves these were the days
before boards you understand the days
long before the King long before Duke

THE NET THROWER

—for Keith Cabral

He returns to the edge
of day to study the dark
mass beneath the surface
of the sea waits and waits
ready to undo life's energy
huddling in tide pools

his own shadow breaks free
thrusts into a dance-move
one arm traces the planets'
arc one leg angles free as if
in flight while the other
roots itself deeply

his own gathered mass
of knotted intersections long
held back draped over his arm
now float aloft rippling releasing
their geometric waves

if I could only capture such
moments release my twists
and turns of ink cast webs
of words to fall upon unsuspecting
synchronicities land them shining
on the page caught up
wriggling to get free

FISHING THE HŌʻEA FLATS

—for Jeff Coakley

The shoulders of Kohala
lean into the waters as if
they're gently pushing lava
tumbled down so long ago
this place where wind meets
no obstacle where man and son
step to the edge with curiosity
purpose filled with winter's
stories of perch nenue kole
and uhu lighting their way
across the shards of past lives
the small pieces of scattered
jigsaw puzzle grandmothers
lived inside but the two men
don't take the serious path
the one they left up on Akoni
Pule Highway where there is much
getting and spending this day they
are light of heart and filled
with the excited voices of those
who came before—those who
first broke the surface and began
to understand the secrets beneath

SHARD

—for Kenji

Today in the gravel at Kenji's place
I find myself outside the house of one
who combed the shorelines of Kohala
a land once covered in sugar plantations
canes cut down for the world's sweet cravings
I found not a stone but a made thing
a small keepsake a thumb-sized fractal
a white porcelain piece of a bowl
thrown by a potter on another
island perhaps off the coast of Kyushu
a cross-hatching all that remains of the blue
house where she once waited
for his return the glaze a thin study
of what once endured for the heart
a traveler wagon wheels horseback
who knows about that long voyage
into the rising sun to these islands
at 20 degrees latitude these shards
broken like her heart like this bowl
that once served so well a man who
stayed worked hard never returned

NO TRACE

Last seen walking an isolated beach low tide
remote island maybe an eye witness made up
this story the way she leaned into him
hands loosely clasped knees lifting in
certain mystic synchronicity his trouser legs
unrolled wet around the ankles feet
immersed in trembling shallow surf
a zephyr pink imbuing even her white
shift wet too the hem clinging all this
just a moment just an image in and out
of focus deciding hesitating long since
given up let go whatever each brought
lost while history rewrites itself and over
here this side behind our left shoulder
someone says it doesn't matter but there
was a coincidence I hear you say an address
in Chicago an elderly aunt en route to Santa Barbara
a garden with fireflies and a night without traffic
without urgency only the pale undoing of
corn in the kettle meat searing and laughter
never talk of the throbbing aircraft their
endless migrations dropping fire afar
so much pain washed away in this tide

THE TRANSFER STATION

"If you see your neighbor carrying something, help him with his load, but don't go mistaking paradise for that home across the road."—Bob Dylan

When I arrive at the dump, officially known as the transfer station, there's already a guy there, a thin, bent-over guy I've seen around. He's wearing Wellington boots and his age doesn't stop him from clambering around the bed of his dark red pickup truck. After parallel parking next to him with about half my pickup bed open to the drop, I start to tidy up the end of one of his ropes that's fallen on the ground and he waves me off. I follow this with a question about what to do with a couple of spools of weed-eater nylon line that I can't use. I'm wondering if I should just set these on the side. I mean, there's turquoise and a range of fluorescent reds and sizes but he chops the air towards the abyss as if to say throw it in! Get rid of it! You brought it this far: go for it! Then he speaks. Use your own judgment.

All the way home I thought of those four words: Use your own judgment. Thought back on all the movement in my life that began in hesitation, asking others what they think, what they would do, looking to the other for advice, decision-making magic, or some kind of childlike craving for the nod of approval. What the hell? Make it okay before it even happens? I've consoled myself all these years believing in caution. It's not hesitation, it's consideration, care and concern before taking the first step. What are we talking about here? …concrete images please…if there's one thing transfer stations deal in, it's concrete images…

Okay Foley, you don't need permission any more: Your call.

I wish.

But it didn't stop there. As he empties his truck I think Oh well, he's a loner, just keep on keeping on.... But he's no sooner finished with his truck than he literally leaps into mine, and commences dragging all the stuff from the cab-end down to me and I'm holding my hands up, saying No, no, no, I didn't even help you....but here comes all my stuff...what is this? I did what many of us who move to the islands do, I explain away any difficulties I might have understanding what's going on with the phrase "cultural difference." Which could sound dangerously like, "He's weird and I'm normal."

"Transfer station" is a waste management practice. It's a place where rubbish is collected prior to its being taken to its final destination, the real dump over in Hilo, the landfill. But island life being what it is, other things besides rubbish get brought to this place, personal foibles being top of the list. Vehicles can be lined either side of the chainlink fenced entrance, taking turns to get close to the rubbish drop, and suddenly a car, or worse, a truck, speeds through the gate and does their thing while the rest of us sit and wait even longer. But I'm not thinking of The Golden Rule, which does help, especially when a group of folks who don't know each other have to wait their turn. I'm thinking of that wiry guy who wouldn't let me help him and then insisted on helping me. I'm thinking of that final place where my normal and your normal face off.

THE GOOD NEIGHBOR

I

It's an ancient mythological landscape
with people falling from the sky a farmer
works the soil on the headland a stagehand
in a multi-colored shirt lands at the mouth
of his driveway and waits for his wife who's
retrieving rosebud and tuberose lei from
the fridge back at the house when a black
pickup truck cuts through this scene with
red brake lights burning up the curve of
the hill and the white arc of a tumbling
trash bag scattering what's left of a celebration
down the center line and at that moment
only the wind speaks up sending paper
plates rolling uphill as if to say this party's
not over but the black truck's driver made
the wrong decision because a neighbor enters
with his big red diesel truck right through
napkins plastic forks and cake-smeared
plates bouncing around the road then he
leaps onto the road himself says "Somebody
had a birthday party!" and plucks a plate
from the air grabs the bag now half full
and starts speeding up the action and for
what it's worth the man in the shirt can't
stand and watch so he too grabs at stray
pieces of somebody else's good times
gone bad as they make their getaway and he
notes the cake with white icing and blue

decorations all that's left going back
in the bag now thrown in the back of
the neighbor's truck as those two nod
to each other without shaking sticky hands
in this timeless scene that will play over
and over until someone paints it so we
can tell this story how some of us won't
walk away from other people's mistakes
and you won't see it in the newspapers
or on TV or in the textbooks or city records
or the internet café flickering with the latest
self-indulgent phantasmagoria and yet
there's something timeless about this scene
something about how we got this far and how
if we're going to keep on going
this is how

These two poems are dedicated to my neighbor, Robert Medeiros. My wife
read the first version of The Good Neighbor and said, You have to give it to
Robert—the neighbor in the poem. Then she laughed. But you have to write
it like a country western song! Before I handed him a copy, I read this country
western version aloud to Robert on the steps outside the Hāwī Post Office.

II

One bright Sunday morning
without any warning
a black truck came racing
down our country hill

and as he went flying
at a speed death-defying
part of his trash load
went for a spill

his brakes they went bright red
we all thought he'd stop dead
and back up and pick up
and show some good-will

but he kept on going
without hardly slowing
and left all his rubbish
and nothing but ill

I stood hesitating
because I was waiting
to go out all fancy
to the best breakfast grill

when who should I see
coming out of his driveway
my neighbor who looked twice
when he saw that spill

he backed right up to it
and I've got to admit
I admired him for stopping
and showing good-will

"Somebody's birthday!"
's what I heard him say
as he moved up the road
with a bag he would fill

when I saw his good deed
I picked up his lead
and chased paper plates
blowing right up our hill

and when we were through
both of us knew
we couldn't walk away
it just wouldn't pay
no matter what you say
about that asshole's spill

TAPS

There's something honest about this morning
the way the world carried on through our sleep
I stand at the open front door watching trees
bend west as if pushed by the rising sun itself
somebody touches my shoulder and my cup
grows cold I still hear voices come through
the radio fallen daughters fallen sons in another
time zone a bugle sounding day's close a lullaby
rocking that other night back into this sunrise
two white flocks of windswept egrets beat
against the blue I've already put the flag out
for the expected delivery there's nothing left
except hold on to the threshold and cry

FOR KINDY

—for Cheryl Sproat

Take Puʻu Hue Road as far as the cattle guard
When the trades slacken you can see pearly reflections
Clouds sail the ocean below and a speck appears to be a barge
Cattle spread out like black birds on the flanks of the mountain

Trades slacken till you can see pearly reflections
Back in town the procession makes its way towards Niuliʻi
Cattle graze here like black birds on the mountain
Gone from his porch at Pololū our living treasure

The procession makes its way Hāwī Kapaʻau Halaʻula Makapala
Breathe deep the updrafts risen from the valley
Gone from his porch at Pololū our living treasure
I'm not alone when I say his voice will never die

Breathe deep the updrafts rising from the valley
Endless lines of travelers whisper
We're not alone and his voice will never die
In wind or stillness in Kohala

Endless lines of friends and family whisper
Clouds sail the ocean below and the barge disappears from view
Wind or stillness in Kohala
Head on down beyond the cattle guard at Puʻu Hue

You're not alone because his voice will never die

QUESTIONS

The air cool at my feet
comes in the open window
falls to the floor
outside light grows
every leaf waits
we all expect day
a car engine on the mountain road
the creaking of my gut with the descent of one espresso
a little water a chocolate biscotti the old ladies
humming and hawing through their beaks
stirring in this growing light
what light's growing in me I wonder
what hemming and hawing what humming
as I settle my breath in one corner
electric light over one shoulder
I point my pen again and again
I've got so many questions
vague swirling roomsful
of questions
I've got grey dawn
gardensful of questions hanging
heavy lidded congested thick headed
half way down the page somewhere
between sacred and profane questions
questions that will never get answered
questions that come down from the shelf
shrug and grunt go back straightened
erect sorts of questions questions
with spines lines signs

questions that hang in the mouth
on the lips
determined to have a good time
quests with no ending

TAKÁCS-YANG

For the record, the Takác's Quartet traveled at least 3300 miles from their homes in Boulder, Colorado to the Island of Hawai'i & Joyce Yang journeyed almost 5000 miles from New York City for this performance in the Kahilu Theatre, Waimea.

Even my big black truck's windshield wipers made music
while I peered through the smears at the lines on the mountain road

First they played Haydn's *Rider Quartet* and we tried to sit still
but applause broke out between movements and the cellist smiled

Next was tricky, Bartok's number five, arching dissonance
and spooky sounds of night mixed in with a melancholy or longing

At intermission, the retired bookseller said he liked the first one—
the second, too raucous. I thought of the miles the quartet had travelled

Dvorak's piano quintet with the young feisty pianist came last
forty-five minutes that lasted three days or a rapid plunk on the viola

We stood right away, we cheered, we roared and shouted for more
you know how greedy we get who cares how far they came

PARADISE IN FOURTEEN LINES

Over the sea and far away
the seven sailing stars above
clouds encircle islands like a lei
and whales still talk of love
some travelers stay awhile then leave
while some folk find a home at last
some give back more than they receive
some say they used to move too fast
paradoxically this place called paradise
is deceptively slow and easy at first
but life's on the edge and a word to the wise
before your endless vacation bubbles burst
never turn your back on the ocean
and watch out for the goddess of lava in motion

RAINBOW

—for Jessica Bliss

First of all believe
there's no up no
down no right side
wrong side out of
bed or in your brain

though every rainbow
smiles for those who
stand on their heads
it's as easy as picking up
love with chopsticks

as crazy as color red
orange yellow green blue
indigo violet feeling their way
through every raindrop
between you and the sun

can you taste those prismatic
displays will you weigh my
word for it? all those rays!
can joy be explained? can
the world still work miracles?

YOU ARE THE RAINWATER

You are the rainwater caught
in the jaws of the blue agave
I am the thirsty black cat
consuming you drop by drop

ABOUT THE AUTHOR

Michael Foley was born in London, England, to Irish parents. He has worked as a stagehand and school teacher. His writing includes free lance research, poetry and memoir. His work has been published in *Sightlines Journal of British Theatre Technicians*, *Resurgence* magazine, *Methuen's Anthology of Theatre Verse* and small press publications such as *Trillium*, *Lookout* and *Fireweed*. His poetry is collected in *Watching the Egg Dance in the Pan* and most recently, *Hair of the Barista*, available on Amazon. A second chapbook of poems written in Malaga, titled *Beauty It Turns Out*, is forthcoming. A memoir from his year as a stagehand in Stratford-Upon-Avon with the Royal Shakespeare Theatre continues to be a work in progress. He has lived in Kohala on Hawaiʻi Island since 2001. He is a member of Na Kupuna O Kohala hula halau.

Made in United States
Troutdale, OR
09/05/2023

12657541R00099